~EX LIBRIS~

Cannella
847-451-6044

Parenting

Wit&Wisdom

Parenting

Wit&Wisdom

FROM

Barbara Coloroso

Highlights
from her
internationally
bestselling books
kids are worth it!
and **Parenting
through Crisis**

PENGUIN

VIKING

VIKING
Published by the Penguin Group
Penguin Books Canada Ltd, 10 Alcorn Avenue, Toronto, Ontario,
Canada M4V 3B2
Penguin Books Ltd, 80 Strand, London WC2R 0RL, England
Penguin Putnam Inc., 375 Hudson Street, New York, New York 10014, U.S.A.
Penguin Books Australia Ltd, Ringwood, Victoria, Australia
Penguin Books (NZ) Ltd, cnr Rosedale and Airborne Roads, Albany,
Auckland 1310, New Zealand

Penguin Books Ltd, Registered Offices: Harmondsworth, Middlesex, England

First published 2001

1 3 5 7 9 10 8 6 4 2

Copyright © Barbara Coloroso, 2001
Illustrations © Joey Coloroso, 2001

Printed and bound in Canada on acid free paper ∞

NATIONAL LIBRARY OF CANADA CATALOGUING IN PUBLICATION DATA

Coloroso, Barbara
Parenting wit & wisdom from Barbara Coloroso

ISBN 0-670-04301-x

1. Child rearing.   I. Title.

HQ769.C62   2001   649'.1   C2001-902665-x

Visit Penguin Canada's website at www.penguin.ca

To Yumi, Mason, and Duncan,
I wish for each one of you the gentle joy
that comes with justice seeking and peacemaking.

A heartfelt thanks to my son, Joseph,
for capturing in art the essence of my words.

Because they are children and for no other reason
they have dignity and worth,
simply because they are . . .

—BARBARA COLOROSO

Note to Parents

Parenting Wit and Wisdom is a compilation of highlights from *kids are worth it! Giving your child the gift of inner discipline* and *Parenting through Crisis: helping kids in times of loss, grief, and change. kids are worth it!* offers practical advice for parents of toddlers through teenagers on how to utilize the very stuff of family life—chores, mealtime, sibling rivalry, toilet training, bedtime, allowances—to create a home environment in which kids can develop their own sense of inner discipline. When these routines are overshadowed by tragic or traumatic events, when children are faced with life's chaos and confusion, the lessons learned through these opportunities do not go to waste. Knowing how to think, not just what to think; feeling empowered, not controlled or manipulated; being able to distinguish between realities that must be accepted and problems that can be solved; and being able to act with compassion and integrity—these are skills that will serve your children well as they navigate the turbulent waters of adversity and sorrow.

If used in the good times, the tools of good parenting—treating kids with respect; giving them a sense of positive power in their own lives; giving them opportunities to make decisions, take responsibility for their actions, and learn from their successes and mistakes—are the same tools you can use in the rough times.

But you will need more. Suffering is a natural part of life and we cannot eliminate it. What we can eliminate are the things we do to unnecessarily compound our own suffering, and the things we do to unnecessarily cause others to suffer. *Parenting through Crisis* is a journey through the inevitable suffering that is a part of living and a journal of ways to approach with compassion and optimism some of life's most daunting situations. It is also a guide to using reconciliatory justice for handling serious mistakes, mischief, and mayhem that happen in our homes and our communities.

Our Parenting Toolbox

There are no quick fixes, easy answers, or recipes for parenting, but I believe most of us have the tools we need to be good parents if only we could find them. Our problem is that these tools are often covered over at the bottom of our mental toolboxes. The tools that come first to hand do not serve us well. These tools were given to us, often unintentionally and without malice, by our parents, grandparents, siblings, and extended family, as well as by our society. Often, when a hammer would best serve our needs, we reach into the toolbox and come out with a hatchet without realizing it. It is no wonder that some of our parenting carpentry is such a mess.

To get the tools we need, we must first become aware of the inappropriate, ineffective, or destructive tools that we are using. Then we must be willing to let go of the old tools and begin using those that can serve us and our children better. Before identifying and sorting the tools, it helps to know what kind of mental toolbox we are using to carry them around.

The toolbox is defined by the answers to two basic questions:

1. What is my parenting philosophy?
2. What is my goal in parenting—to influence and empower my children or to control them and make them mind?

If we know our own philosophy, we can examine various parenting tools, including those we are using right now. If a tool doesn't fit with our philosophy, regardless of who said it or what kind of research is behind it, we can choose not to use it. I have found three tenets to be the most useful in evaluating my own and other people's recommended parenting techniques:

1. Kids are worth it.
2. I will not treat a child in a way I myself would not want to be treated. If I wouldn't want it done to me, I have no business doing it to my child.
3. If it works, and leaves a child's and my own dignity intact, do it. Just because it works doesn't make it good; it must work and leave the child's and my own dignity intact.

Kids Are Worth It!

Because they are children and for no other reason they have dignity and worth, simply because they are. They don't need to prove their value as human beings; they don't have to prove their worthiness to us; nor do they need to earn our affection.

Believing that kids are worth it also means believing that our neighbour's kids are worth it. As adults we need to be willing to make the sacrifices necessary to ensure that all children in our community will be able to have what they need: proper medical treatment; food, clothing, and shelter; opportunities to explore, grow, and be nurtured in a safe environment. This is too much for one individual to do, but it is definitely possible if as a society we believe that our kids are worth the time, energy, resources, and commitment necessary to help them become responsible, resourceful, resilient, and compassionate human beings.

I Will Not Treat a Child in a Way I Myself Would Not Want to Be Treated

The ethic that we should treat others as we ourselves want to be treated and not in a way we ourselves would not want to be treated is found in all the great religions of the world. The Golden Rule, as it is called, can serve us well when applied to our relations with our children. If we are not sure whether what we are doing with children is right, we need only put ourselves in their place and ask if we would want it done to us—not was it done to us, but would we want it done to us? If the answer is no, then we have to ask ourselves why we would ever want to do it to our children.

It is not enough merely to ask if I would want it done to me if I were in my child's shoes. As good a check of a parenting tool as that question is, we must go one step further and consider the consequences of our actions.

If It Works, and Leaves a Child's and My Own Dignity Intact, Do It

Just because a parenting tool works or appears to work doesn't make it a good one. An unintended consequence of using tools that control kids and make them mind is that "good behaviour" is purchased at a terrible cost—that is, at the expense of the dignity and self-worth of both the parent and the child.

If we want to raise children who have a strong sense of inner discipline, who don't act merely to please someone or to avoid punishment but who behave in a responsible and compassionate way toward themselves and others because it is the right thing to do, then we must abandon some "tried and true" parenting tools of the past and reject some of the more recent alternatives.

Physical punishment is an obvious form of abuse. Not so obvious and often overlooked forms of abuse are emotional battering and neglect. When children hear constant criticism and putdowns, they begin to see themselves as not good enough or just plain bad.

Some children are neglected by their parents. They may have all the material possessions they could want, but no nurturing, cuddling, or warm words of encouragement—only coldness. The deep sense of loss and grief doesn't show up in bruises or broken bones but in a broken heart—a hopelessness and despair that affects their marriages, their connections as family, their work, and their play.

The profound consequences of such abuse can give us pause to reflect on all of the tools we use. Some tools that appear to be better than punishment are indeed merely the flip side of the same coin. If we praise children instead of putting them down, reward them for good deeds instead of hitting them for mistakes or mischief, replace the paddle with an offer of a trip to the park if they don't hit their brother, we must ask ourselves if we aren't still trying to control our children and "make" them mind, just doing it in a "nicer" way. What are the consequences to our children, our family, and our community if we raise children to "do to please," to do what they are told to do, and to help others only if there is something in it for them?

Those of us committed to making a change must fight the demons from within, for we carry in our mental toolboxes destructive tools that are well-worn family heirlooms, passed on from generation to generation. The first step to rid ourselves of them is committing to the three basic philosophical tenets. The next step is to ask, "What is my goal in parenting?—to influence and empower my children, or to control them and make them mind?"

Power and Influence

Power is like a candle with a huge flame. The beauty of empowering another human being is that we never lose our own power in the process. In fact, we will have a greater light to see by. And in old age, when our flame starts to flicker—and it will—we will have the next generation's light to guide us.

Empowering our children involves first giving them a secure, safe, nurturing environment—offering them unconditional love, caring touch, tenderness, and concern for their physical, emotional, and spiritual well-being. Within that environment, children can begin to make choices and decisions and mistakes, assume responsibilities and become actively involved family members. Engaging them in critical reflection, teaching them always to be aware of the consequences of their actions on others, showing them how to accept responsibility for their accomplishments and mistakes—all this empowers them to become responsible, resilient, resourceful, compassionate individuals who can act in their own best interests, stand up for themselves, and exercise their own rights while respecting the rights and legitimate needs of others.

Three Kinds of Families

Brick-wall and jellyfish families, although at opposite extremes, tend to raise children who know what to think but not how to think or feel, and who lack a sense of a true self. They have neither faith in themselves nor hope for the future and are therefore at risk of damage or destruction from the three horsemen of the adolescent apocalypse: sexual promiscuity, drug abuse, and suicide. Neither family provides the structure a child can use as a backbone for developing mentally, physically, sexually, emotionally, and morally. Both families can produce children who as adults will believe themselves to be powerless and unable to live truly satisfying lives.

Backbone families are characterized not so much by what they do or don't do but how they balance the sense of self and the sense of community in all that they do. Interdependence is celebrated.

Backbone families can also be described by what they are not: they are not hierarchical, bureaucratic, or violent. Parents don't demand respect—they demonstrate and teach it. Children learn to question and challenge authority that is not life-giving. They learn that they can say no, that they can listen and be listened to, that they can be respectful and be respected themselves. Children are taught empathy and love for themselves and others. By being treated with compassion themselves they learn to be compassionate toward others, to recognize others' suffering, and to be willing to help relieve it.

The backbone family provides the consistency, firmness, and fairness as well as the calm and peaceful structure needed for children to flesh out their own sense of true self. Rather than being subjected to power expressed as control and growing up to control others, children are empowered and grow up to pass what they have learned of the potential of the human spirit on to others. Such families help children develop inner discipline, and even in the face of adversity and peer pressure, they retain faith in themselves and their own potential.

Brick-Wall Family Checklist

1. Hierarchy of control.
2. Litany of strict rules.
3. Punctuality, cleanliness, and order.
4. Rigid enforcement of rules by means of actual threatened or imagined violence.
5. Attempt to break the child's will and spirit with fear and punishment.
6. Rigid rituals and rote learning.
7. Use of humiliation.
8. Extensive use of threats and bribes.
9. Heavy reliance on competition.
10. Learning takes place in an atmosphere of fear.
11. Love is highly conditional.
12. Separate and strictly enforced roles for boys and girls.
13. Teach what to think, not how to think.
14. Risk of sexual promiscuity, drug abuse, and suicide.
15. Refuse to acknowledge the need to get help.

Jellyfish Family Checklist

1. Anarchy and chaos in the physical and emotional environment.
2. No recognizable structure, rules, and guidelines.
3. Arbitrary and instant punishments and rewards.
4. Minilectures and putdowns are tools of the trade.
5. Second chances are arbitrarily given.
6. Threats and bribes are commonplace.
7. Everything takes place in an environment of chaos.
8. Emotions rule the behaviour of parents and children.
9. Children are taught that love is highly conditional.
10. Children are easily led by their peers.
11. Risk of sexual promiscuity, drug abuse, and suicide.
12. Parents are oblivious to major family problems and fail to recognize the need to seek help.

Backbone Family Checklist

1. Parents develop for their children a network of support through six critical life messages given every day.
2. Democracy is learned through experience.
3. An environment is created that is conducive to creative, constructive, and responsible activity.
4. Rules are simple and clearly stated.
5. Consequences for irresponsible behaviour are either natural or reasonable, simple, valuable, and purposeful (RSVP).
6. Discipline is handled with authority that gives life to children's learning.
7. Children are motivated to be all they can be.
8. Children receive lots of smiles, hugs, and humour.
9. Children get second opportunities.

10. Children learn to accept their own feelings and to act responsibly on those feelings through a strong sense of self-awareness.
11. Competency and cooperation are modelled and encouraged.
12. Love is unconditional.
13. Children are taught how to think.
14. Children are buffered from sexual promiscuity, drug abuse, and suicide by the daily reinforcement of the messages that foster self-esteem:

    I like myself

    I can think for myself

    There is no problem so great, it can't be solved.
15. The family is willing to seek help.

Threats, Punishment, Bribes, and Rewards

Threats, punishment, bribes, and rewards are so common in our culture that we rarely question their efficacy. These four tools do work. They also keep a child dependent and fearful—dependent on a parent for rewards given for positive behaviour, and fearful of whatever punishment that same parent might mete out for negative behaviour. They work when our goal is to get children to do what we want them to do.

If, however, our goal is different—if we want our children to become ethical, compassionate, creative, competent individuals who have a strong sense of self, know how to think and not just what to think, who are naturally curious about themselves and the world around them, who don't "do to please" and are not easily led, who are willing to act with integrity—then these four tools do not work. Children have a difficult time becoming responsible, resourceful, and resilient if they are controlled, manipulated, and made to mind, robbed of their autonomy and denied opportunities to make choices and mistakes. They cannot develop a sense of inner discipline if all of the control comes from the outside.

The Problems with Threats and Punishments

1. Impose control from without, arouse resentment, and invite more conflict.
2. Preempt more constructive ways of relating to a child and avoid dealing with the underlying causes of conflict.
3. Discourage children from acknowledging their actions.
4. Deprive children of the opportunity to understand the consequences of their actions, fix what they did, or empathize with the people they may have harmed.
5. Help children develop a right/wrong, good/bad distorted view of reality.
6. Increase tension in the home.
7. Rob children of their sense of dignity and self-worth.

Threats and punishment can take the form of:

Isolation
Embarrassment and humiliation
Shaming
Emotional isolation
Grounding
Brute force

The use of such negative reinforcement degrades, humiliates, and dehumanizes the children who are its objects. Threats and punishment do nothing to motivate a child to take risks, be creative, or speak up and speak out.

Faced with domination, manipulation, and control by someone bigger than themselves, children will respond in one of three ways:

1. Fear—doing as they are told out of dependency and fear.
2. Fight back—attacking the adult or taking the anger out on others.
3. Flee—running away mentally and physically.

With threats and punishment, children are robbed of the opportunity to develop their own inner discipline—the ability to act with integrity, wisdom, compassion, and mercy when there is no external force holding them accountable for what they do.

The Problems with Bribes and Rewards

1. Implied in the bribe is a threat of the possible loss of the reward.
2. Kids learn to do what they are told without question—not because they believe it is the right thing to do, but to get the reward or avoid the punishment.
3. Kids learn to "do to please."
4. Responsible actions are performed for the payoff, not out of a sense of self-worth, self-control, and self-responsibility.
5. Kids are robbed of the opportunity to take risks, make mistakes, and question adults for fear of losing the promised rewards or losing their parents' goodwill.
6. Kids who "do to please" have no deep understanding of the deeds they have done.
7. Deeds are done merely or mostly for the payoff, and siblings and peers are viewed as obstacles to a child's personal success.

Kids who are consistently bribed and rewarded are likely to grow into adults who are overly dependent on others for approval and recognition, lacking their own self-confidence and sense of responsibility. They frame their deeds in response to the answers to the following questions:

- What's in it for me?
- What's the payoff?
- Does it count for anything?
- Will it get me what I want?
- Do you like it?
- Did you see me do it?
- Did I do it the right way (your way)?

Bribes and rewards can give us temporary compliance, but at the expense of creating less responsible, less resourceful, less resilient, less compassionate young people who will "do to please," are praise-dependent, less generous, and less committed to excellence. These tools train children in selfishness and greed. Children learn what does and doesn't get them what they want. They ask, "What's in it for me?" not, "What kind of person do I want to be?" The virtues of integrity, honesty, kindness, and compassion become commodities that can be purchased at an ever inflated price.

Bribes and rewards come in all shapes and sizes, each with its own unique ability to manipulate and control. Each is able to rob children of their creativity, autonomy, sense of well-being, and connectedness to those around them. The more any of these are needed or wanted by the child, the greater the potential impact.

The most common forms are:

1. Abundant praise
2. Tangible goodies
3. Our presence as a reward

Kids who are consistently bribed and rewarded will spend a lot of energy trying to figure out what they can do to please (or upset) their parents, and they will have no time or energy left to develop their own capacity to realistically evaluate their own abilities, deeds, and goals.

Pitfalls of Praise

1. Praise can foster and reinforce a sense of insecurity, as children become fearful of not being able to live up to an adult's expectations.
2. Praise that exaggerates accomplishments can invite a child to use a low-risk strategy to avoid failure.
3. Praise can reduce children's confidence in their own answers.
4. Praise can undermine the integrity of the parent/child relationship.
5. Praise can stop a conversation.
6. Praise can invite a rebuttal.
7. Praise can condition children to go for a quick payoff, reducing innovative and complex reasoning.
8. Praise can discourage cooperative learning.
9. Praise that sets up competition gives children the idea that their self-worth and value in the family are contingent on whether they best their siblings or peers.

Is Your Child Reward-Dependent?

The following is a checklist of warning signs that your child might be reward-dependent. Most children will exhibit some of these signs as they struggle to develop their own sense of self. It is the frequency, intensity, and persistence of these behaviours that indicate a need for concern and intervention.

___ 1. "Does to please" to win approval of those in authority.

___ 2. Does what is told to do without questioning.

___ 3. Lacks initiative, waits for orders.

___ 4. Sense of self is defined externally; has dignity and worth when producing what adults want.

___ 5. Who she is and what she does are one and the same. If she does something "bad," she sees herself as "bad."

___ 6. Uses his history as an excuse for his behaviour.

___ 7. Is pessimistic, despairs easily.

___ 8. Places blame outside of self: "He made me do it." "It's not my fault."

___ 9. Hides mistakes, fearful of adults' wrath.

___10. Lies to avoid consequences and cover mistakes.

___11. Feels controlled.

___12. Feels worthwhile only when on top, when number one.

___13. Is competitive, gets ahead at the expense of others.

___14. Needs to be perfect, views mistakes as bad.

___15. Seeks approval and fears disapproval, fearful of rejection.

___16. Is conformist. Goes along with the crowd.

___17. Considers behaviour by its consequences. "If I don't get caught, what I did wasn't wrong."

___18. Focuses on the past and the future, misses the moment. Worries about "what if . . ."

___19. Experiences self-talk that is negative; parental injunctions keep playing over and over.

___20. Has private reservations about public self: "If they really knew me . . ."

___21. Uses only simple problem-solving skills to try to solve all problems.

___22. Is always concerned about the "bottom line."

___23. Says what she thinks others want to hear.

___24. Is cautious, insecure.

___25. Has a mercenary spirit; is selfish, self-centered, greedy, does good deeds to obtain rewards or avoid punishment.

___26. Is cynical and skeptical; views world in terms of "us" and "them."

___27. Swallows values without question from those in authority.

___28. Frames deeds with "should."

___29. Holds on to resentments.

___30. Is oversensitive to criticism, disqualifies compliments.

Is Your Child Responsible, Resourceful, Resilient, and Compassionate?

The following is a checklist of indicators that your child is developing a strong, healthy sense of self.

___ 1. Acts out of a sense of conviction.

___ 2. Makes choices; willing to stand up for a value or against an injustice even in the face of disapproval.

___ 3. Takes initiative; does not wait for an adult to approve or affirm.

___ 4. Has an internally defined sense of self. Lives consciously, purposefully.

___ 5. Accepts responsibility for decisions, choices, and mistakes.

___ 6. Accepts the past, learns from it, and lets it go.

___ 7. Is optimistic. Has realistic expectations, positive outlook.

___ 8. Takes ownership of behaviour and accepts consequences.

___ 9. Takes ownership of mistakes and sees them as opportunities to learn.

___10. Is truthful and realistic.

___11. Feels empowered and self-directed.

___12. Celebrates and cherishes success of self and others.

___13. Is competent, cooperative, decisive; knows own abilities; is willing to share; is open to others' ideas.

___14. Is willing to take risks.

___15. Has a strong sense of self, is open to criticism and compliments, measures both in relation to core identity.

___16. Is self-reliant.

___17. Possesses personal integrity, self-respect.

___18. Experiences life, lives consciously.

___19. Experiences self-talk that is upbeat, realistic, positive, accepting.

___20. Is confident and self-expressive; listens to internal signals (intuitive).

___21. Uses innovative and complex reasoning when appropriate, explores, goes beyond conventional ideas, is creative.

___22. Is playful; everything doesn't have to have a purpose.

___23. Is willing to speak out and share ideas even if not sure how anyone else is going to react.

___24. Is confident, self-assured.

___25. Is altruistic, ethical, and compassionate; attends to others' feelings and points of view.

___26. Has a pro-social orientation, a generalized inclination to share, care, and help.

___27. Examines values before accepting them as own.

___28. Frames deeds with "could."

___29. Lets go of real or perceived hurt.

___30. Can accept criticism and compliments equally well.

The Triangle of Influence—
Encouragement, Feedback,
Discipline

Children cannot thrive on bribes, threats, rewards, and punishments. If you need to get rid of these tools in your parenting toolbox, you can replace them with encouragement, feedback, and discipline.

ENCOURAGEMENT

Encouragement can come at any time. It is nonjudgmental, and it emphasizes the child's importance by expressing confidence and trust in the child. It inspires; it imparts courage and confidence; it gives support. It helps a child develop a sense of self-pride and enhances internal motivation. There is no hint of coercion or desire to control behaviour.

Encouraging a child means that one or more of the six critical life messages are coming through, delivered either by words or by actions:

- I believe in you.
- I trust you.
- I know you can handle this.
- You are listened to.
- You are cared for.
- You are very important to me.

FEEDBACK

Feedback enables kids to look at their expression of feelings, their behaviour, and their deeds honestly and realistically. There are three different kinds of feedback: compliments, comments, and constructive criticism. Each one is an important component in helping kids become responsible, resourceful, and resilient.

1. Compliments are contingent on a child doing something specific. The purpose of them is to recognize persistence, or acknowledge a job well done. They are not flattery, glib positive thinking, or the covering up of unpleasant truths.
2. Comments are neutral feedback as well as basic instructions that can help kids organize and sequence activities. They are intended to instruct, not attack.

3. Constructive criticism specifically attacks the mistake or problem, not the kid. It focuses on actions that kids can change and mistakes that can be fixed.

DISCIPLINE

When we use punishment, our children are robbed of the opportunity to develop their own inner discipline—the ability to act with integrity, wisdom, compassion, and mercy when there is no external force holding them accountable for what they do. Discipline, on the other hand, is not something we do to children. It is a process that gives life to learning; it is restorative, and it invites reconciliation. Its goal is to instruct, to teach, to guide, and to help children develop self-discipline—an ordering of the self from the inside, not an imposition from the outside. In giving life to our children's learning, we are concerned not with mere compliance but with inviting our children to delve deep into themselves and reach beyond what is required or expected.

Discipline takes time. Punishment is so much swifter, rescuing your child so much easier. However, the time you take is well worth it. As she develops her own inner discipline, your child begins to understand that all of her actions have consequences, that she is capable of taking ownership of what she does and that she is just as capable of taking full responsibility for the problems she has created—not because she fears reprisal or punishment, but because it is the right thing to do.

The *process* of discipline does four things that the *act* of punishment cannot do. The steps are:

1. Show children what they have done wrong.
2. Give them ownership of the problem.
3. Help them find ways of solving the problem.
4. Leave their dignity intact.

Discipline involves real-world consequences or intervention, or a combination of the two. It deals with the reality of the situation, not with the control of the adult. Real-world consequences either happen naturally or are reasonable consequences that are intrinsically related to the child's actions.

Just as RSVP is a request for a response, a consequence that is reasonable, simple, valuable, and purposeful will invite a responsible action from your child. When in doubt about a consequence, you can check if all four clues are present:

1. R—Is it reasonable?
2. S—Is it simple?
3. V—Is it valuable as a learning tool?
4. P—Is it purposeful?

If it isn't all four of these, it probably won't be effective and it could be punishment disguised as a reasonable consequence.

Life-Threatening, Morally Threatening, or Unhealthy Consequences

If natural consequences are not life-threatening, morally threatening, or unhealthy, it is good to let a child experience them without warnings or reminders. But if the natural consequences are life-threatening, morally threatening, or unhealthy, as a wise and caring parent you must intervene.

LIFE-THREATENING CONSEQUENCES

Any time a child's life is at risk, there is no question that a parent must intervene. This is no time to teach a child a lesson.

MORALLY THREATENING CONSEQUENCES

Lynn Leight, the author of *Raising Sexually Healthy Children*, puts moral issues in the framework of four answers to the question "Why can't I?"

1. Because it is unkind. (An eight-year-old says she is not going to invite two girls in her class to a birthday party when she is asking all the other girls in the class.)

2. Because it is hurtful. (A four-year-old is holding the family cat by its tail.)
3. Because it is unfair. (A six-year-old keeps taking toys away from a two-year-old, does it "nicely," and leaves the two-year-old bewildered.)
4. Because it is dishonest. (A teenager tells you he is going to take a test for a friend.)

In each of these situations, a parent can take the opportunity to teach the child about the virtues of kindness, compassion, fairness, and honesty and can provide guidance and options for behaving in a virtuous way. It is also a good time to talk with your child about the consequences of her behaviour—not what will happen to her, but what effect her behaviour will have on the other person, on her relationship with that other person, and on herself.

UNHEALTHY CONSEQUENCES

If a child is behaving in a way that would put her health at serious risk, a parent or other caring adult needs to intervene.

If a situation is not life-threatening, morally threatening, or unhealthy, ask yourself if the natural consequence of what your child is doing would give life to your child's learning. If the answer is yes, stay out of it and let nature take its course.

Reconciliatory Justice

Sometimes the four steps of discipline are not enough. When a child makes a mistake or creates mischief that intentionally or unintentionally creates serious problems of great consequence, the three R's of reconciliation are incorporated into the third step of the four steps of discipline—helping find ways to solve the problem. These three R's—Restitution, Resolution, and Reconciliation—provide the tools necessary to begin the healing process when serious material or personal harm has occurred.

THE THREE R's

1. Restitution involves fixing both the physical and personal damage.
2. Resolution involves figuring out ways to keep this from happening again.
3. Reconciliation is the process of healing with the person you have harmed.

Three Alternatives to No

Kids learn not to take us seriously on the big no because we keep changing our minds on the little ones. The following are three alternatives you can start using right away so that when you really need to say no to your kids, they will believe that you mean it.

1. "Yes, later."
2. "Give me a minute."
3. "Convince me."

Self-trust is one of the first steps toward becoming a responsible, resourceful, resilient human being. Children don't need many no's, any minilectures, unnecessary questions, empty threats, ultimatums, putdowns, warnings, or dictates. What they do need is support, explanations, encouragement, opportunities to be responsible, and invitations to think for themselves.

I Can Be Me

Backbone parents offer a network of support through the six critical life messages; they discipline by giving life to their kids' learning; they teach them how to think, not just what to think; they allow and encourage rebellion that is not life-threatening, morally threatening, or unhealthy. The kids say, "I can be me in this family."

An excellent way to teach the art of decision making is to let kids make decisions, guide them through the process without passing judgment, and let them grow through the results of their decisions. Mistakes and poor choices become a child's own responsibility. The hurt or discomfort arising from the choices goes away only after the child has worked out the problem constructively. By having power over the situation, the child's dignity, integrity, and self-worth are enhanced.

Since responsibility and decision making are prerequisites for self-discipline, kids need to be trusted to assume responsibilities and to be given opportunities to make critical decisions throughout their childhood. Responsibilities and decisions need to be age-appropriate and meaningful. Take a critical look at the responsibilities and decision-making opportunities you give your children at home, and check to see if you are increasing them as your kids get older. Keep the ones you need to keep as a wise and caring parent. The rest you can give to your children.

If you invite your children when they are young to express themselves by way of small rebellions, choices, and decisions, as they grow through the third age of rebellion, they will have the backbone on which to flesh out their own identity.

Keeping Your Cool Without Putting Your Feelings on Ice

Kids need to know it's all right to feel. It is all right to be happy, concerned, joyful, sad, angry, frustrated, and hurt. Feelings are motivators for growth or warning signs that something needs changing. When we are concerned or joyful, we have energy to grow and to extend ourselves outward. When we are angry or hurt, our feelings are signalling our mind and body that something is not right and needs to be changed. Sometimes what needs changing is not the situation itself but our view of it.

In jellyfish families kids are not taught how to identify or responsibly express their feelings. Often the adults express their own feelings and respond to their child's feelings in extreme ways. The parent will either smother the child and try to own the feelings for her, not encouraging her to work through her own feelings and protecting her from the consequences of the expression of her feelings. Or the parent will totally disregard the child's feelings through abandonment or neglect.

In brick-wall families, where parents demand obedience and rule by fear, kids are taught at a very young age not to express their true feelings. Spontaneous expressions of joy, concern, and happiness are stifled because all feelings are stifled by the parents. Anger, hostility, opposition, and sadness are all punished. Eventually the child becomes so wary of her parents that no feelings are spontaneously expressed; she must first "check in" with her parents to see if the feeling is okay. Forbidden to express these emotions themselves, kids get stuck in their anger, fear, sadness, and hurt. Sometimes they even refuse to acknowledge that they are angry or hurt and have no way of getting rid of the energy produced by those feelings. The energy builds up inside, like steam pressure in a boiler.

Eventually one of three things results:

1. Passive-destructive acts against the self.
2. Aggressive acts against others.
3. Passive-aggressive acts (a combination of the other two).

Parents in a backbone family regularly do five things:

1. They acknowledge their own feelings and label them.
2. They admit that they are angry, or hurt, or afraid, then do something responsible and purposeful to address these feelings.
3. They make assertive statements about themselves.
4. They acknowledge their children's feelings as real and legitimate, without passing judgment on those feelings.
5. They teach their children to handle their own feelings assertively.

The Temper Tantrum

Temper tantrums happen—they are not planned. Parents can anticipate them intelligently, or they can fear them and then ignore them when they happen. Neither approach will prevent the tantrum, and the second approach will often make it worse. But understanding the causes of tantrums will help parents anticipate when one is about to happen.

Tantrums usually occur when kids are tired, hungry, frustrated, or all three. If parents remain calm, they can help their children by eliminating the cause or by redirecting the energy in a more responsible and productive way.

Often when they are on the verge of a major break-through in their physical, mental, or psychological development, kids will become very agitated, frustrated, sullen, or angry. Just before he learns to walk, or she takes off on the two-wheeler, or he learns to combine letters to make words, or she begins to menstruate, temper tantrums seem to be the norm of the day, with calm and reason but a passing memory.

Tough as it is, it is easier to be patient with a two-year-old who is throwing a temper tantrum than with a teenager doing the same thing. Yet he needs the same help labelling his feelings and figuring out constructive ways to handle them. It takes time to teach kids to handle their feelings assertively, but in doing so you teach them that their own feelings are important, that they can be trusted to handle those feelings, and that they can count on you for support and guidance when they have handled them poorly.

Seven Steps for a Fair Fight

Confrontation is sometimes necessary, but all too often it means endless arguments that waste a great deal of energy, lead only to further argument, and solve nothing. Kids need to learn better ways. In order to confront effectively, they must first understand their anger:

- Where did it come from? (From inside myself.)
- Is it masking another feeling? (I am hurt, or frustrated, or disappointed, or afraid.)
- Why be angry anyway? (Because I care. If I didn't care, I wouldn't be angry. I can't be angry about something I don't care about, with someone I don't care about.)

Once the anger is understood, kids are prepared to confront the person they are angry with.

1. When you are upset or angry, say so in an upset or angry tone of voice. Let your whole body speak the message in a straightforward, assertive manner—not aggressively or passively.
2. Tell the other person about your feelings.
3. State your belief out loud but avoid killer statements.

4. Close the time gap between the hurt and the expression of that hurt. Give direct feedback.
5. State what you want from the other person.
6. Be open to the other person's perspective on the situation.
7. Negotiate an agreement you can both accept.

Both children and adults need to recognize that to keep it a fair fight, it is always acceptable to

1. Call time out.
2. Refuse to take abuse.
3. Insist on fair treatment.

We need to help our children learn to recognize when it is necessary to call time out, to know they have the right not to be verbally or physically abused by anyone and that they have the right to be treated with respect, dignity, and fairness. They also have the responsibility not to let their feelings take over a situation, to see that they do not physically, verbally, or emotionally abuse another person, and to treat other people with the same respect and dignity they themselves ask for. Fighting fair enables parents and kids to use their feelings as a positive energy source to establish and maintain productive relationships with one another and with other people outside the family.

Realities, Mistakes, and Problems

How our children learn to deal with life has a lot to do with how we as parents view life and handle our own mistakes and problems. Our attitude, as well as our action, is important. If we are optimistic, we seek solutions to our problems; if we are pessimistic, we seek someone to blame.

A backbone parent admits that she made a mistake, takes full responsibility for making the mistake, avoids making excuses, figures out how to fix the problem created by making the mistake, recognizes if and how another person was affected, and figures out what to do the next time so it won't happen again. By taking ownership, she shows her children a way to accept responsibility for their own mistakes.

You often can't control what happens to you, but what you *can* do is control how you use what is happening to you. A big part of using what is happening to you is distinguishing between what can be changed and what has to be accepted.

WHOSE PROBLEM

Before starting to solve a problem, it is critical to know who owns it. If you are going to solve a problem, first make sure it is yours to solve. Most of the time it does neither of you any good if you solve someone else's problem. However, sometimes logic and emotion send two different signals to your head. You know you shouldn't rescue your child from the mess he created himself, but it would be so much simpler and more efficient to get him out of a mess just this one time; and besides, he'll love you more (or dislike you less) if you take care of the problem for him. These two signals are warnings that you need to pause and question the messages you are giving your child by rushing in and solving the problem for him.

The opposite of rescuing—washing your hands of any involvement in your kid's problems, even when she is in way over her head and really needs your help and support—also confuses and complicates the issue of who owns a problem. It sends a message to your child that you will not be there when she really needs you.

43

INTUITION

Intuition is your inner self speaking and reaching out. It often provides options that aren't immediately obvious to your logical mind or your emotional heart. Being able to acknowledge, trust, and act on intuition is essential to a harmonious, healthy life and is particularly useful when you are faced with complex difficulties and problems. If listened to, intuition can often point the way out of an impasse that thinking and emotion have only confused. Your intuition helps you to know when to reach out and when to refrain from reaching out, when to speak and when to be silent, when to hold on and when to let go. You are no longer merely logical or emotional. Connecting your head and heart to your intuition, you are able to respond to your children mindfully and with a wise heart.

Six Steps to Problem Solving

1. Identify and define the problem.
2. List viable options for solving the problem.
3. Evaluate the options—explore the pluses and minuses for each option.
4. Choose one option.
5. Make a plan and DO IT.
6. Evaluate the problem and your solution: What brought it about? Could a similar problem be prevented in the future? How was the present problem solved?

Family Meetings

A family meeting can be a forum for kids to learn to examine situations, propose solutions, and evaluate the results with guidance, support, and demonstrations from parents and older siblings. It is an opportunity to reinforce the notion that the goal for our children is not dependence or independence but rather a sense of interdependence.

There are three basic requirements for such a meeting:

1. The problem must be important and relevant to all concerned.
2. The parent needs to provide nonjudgmental leadership.
3. The environment needs to be conducive to sharing.

In a family meeting, problems are stated simply and clearly, then clarified. All family members look at various options and discuss the feasibility of their choices.

Solutions are proposed, and a plan of action is agreed upon and carried out. The results are then evaluated.

Having presented their own ideas, listened to one another's reasoning, and worked cooperatively to arrive at a solution, all family members begin to see that there is no definite right or wrong, no one correct way to solve most problems. Group choices involve give and take, openness, and cooperation on the part of all concerned. Everyone feels that they are listened to, cared for, and important. The skills learned in family meetings will help kids deal effectively with problems they may have in other social settings.

Getting Your Kid Out of Jail and Other Mega-Problems

Simply because our teenagers have free will and are subject to one of the strongest forces in the universe—peer pressure—many of us parents may have to deal with mega-problems our teens have created for themselves. Although more difficult to handle than clothes left on the floor, mega-problems are still solvable.

As their whole world is crashing in on them, what teens need is someone to stand behind them and tell them, "I believe in you. I trust you. I know you can handle this. You are listened to, cared for, and very important to me. We love you and we're here—not to rescue, blame, or punish but to support and discipline." It's vital to remember the last, discipline, because without it, help can easily turn into rescuing.

When your teen is in serious trouble with the law, along with the necessary legal counsel it is important to get professional advice and support for both of you. Counsellors trained in dealing with troubled teens and their families can help you get at the core of the problem as well as address the immediate offense. They can also be there to give you and your teen a hug, a shoulder to cry on, and options for solving the mega-problems, while brick-wall members of the community push to "throw the book" at him and jellyfishes try to find excuses for his behaviour.

Don't Tell Alice When She's Ten Feet Tall—What to Do When You Suspect Your Teenager Is Doing Drugs

If your teen has a drug problem, she has a better chance of solving it if you are an aware and involved parent. Partnership for a Drug-Free America gives the following signs to look for:

THE TELLTALE SIGNS

Chronic eye redness, sore throat, or dry cough
Chronic lying, especially about whereabouts
Wholesale changes in friends
Stealing
Deteriorating relationships with family members
Wild mood swings, hostility, or abusive behaviour
Chronic fatigue, withdrawal, carelessness about personal
    grooming
Major changes in eating or sleeping patterns
Loss of interest in favourite activities, hobbies, sports
School problems—slipping grades, absenteeism

OTHER WARNING SIGNS

Drug slogans on clothes
Language laced with drug terminology

Having lots of money or no money and no reasonable
    accounting for either
Hysterical crying or hysterical laughter
Paranoid behaviour
Incense burning

DIRECT EVIDENCE OF DRUG USE

Drug paraphernalia
Marijuana plants, seeds, or leaves
Actual drugs or evidence of drugs
Drug odours
Needle tracks, skin boils, and sores
Sniffing gasoline, glue, solvents, or aerosol

When confronted with the signs of possible drug use by
your teen, you first accept the possibility that it is true,
recognize that it is her problem to work through, and then
commit to being there for her over the long haul.

The Premier National Law Enforcement Publishing
Company, in their booklet *Children and Drugs—The Next
Generation*, lists ten steps a parent can take:

1. Don't panic or react out of anger or fear.
2. Make yourself as knowledgeable about drugs as you
   can: check with your local library, local drug-related
   assistance programs, school authorities, etc. Remember
   also that your children may know a great deal.

3. Determine who has the best rapport with your child (it may not be you) and ask his or her assistance. Keep the lines of communication open.

4. Commence a "low key" dialogue to determine why and how the child reached a decision to use drugs or what brought him to use drugs. Remember, the involvement may be brief and experimental; don't back him into a corner by prejudging, threatening, or moralizing.

5. Drug use, or heavy involvement in drugs, may well be symptomatic of other problems perhaps more urgent. Don't ignore them or think them irrelevant.

6. Involve others along the way if this seems appropriate, preferably with the voluntary approval of the child. Be careful in your selection. Use persons or services that specialize in treatment of drug or alcohol abuse.

7. Be honest and factual: accept that the child may bring up inconsistencies or hypocrisies on your part. Don't lose your cool over this.

8. Drugs may be an issue over which your whole relationship with the child may be examined and talked over. It may be a valuable opportunity in many areas.

9. If, in spite of all your efforts, you still consider the problem so serious that more action must be taken, professional or other help should be sought.

10. Remember, if your child is using drugs, some of his friends will be too. Thus there is room for you, along with other parents, to try to offer the whole group something better than drugs.

All of our kids will make mistakes; that's part of growing up. Growing up can be painful, and it's hard for us to see our children in pain. But let the mistakes and poor choices become your kids' own responsibility. That doesn't mean you stand back and let them destroy their lives. If it is life-threatening, morally threatening, or unhealthy, you do step in with loving support and guidance—and sometimes a straightjacket. Just as you might restrain an angry toddler who is hellbent on hurting himself or his younger brother, you might have to get professional help to restrain a drug-crazed son or to intravenously feed an anorexic daughter. The intervention and control is only temporary and will need to give way to the teens' eventually taking ownership of their own problems and the solutions to those problems. The hurt or discomfort arising from their choices goes away only after they have worked out their problems constructively. By having positive power over even such painful situations as mega-problems, their dignity, integrity, and self-worth are enhanced.

Settling Sibling Rivalry
without Calling in the Cavalry

Kids fight. The next time your kids are going at it, take a
big breath and tell yourself, "They're normal." Conflict is
inevitable, as much a part of life as sleeping and eating and
paying taxes. So is the pain that goes along with it. But you
can resolve conflict and make it less painful if you deal
with it directly and creatively.

Knowing how to handle conflict is more than a matter
of creating peace in the home; it is a matter of creating a
peaceful attitude in ourselves and our children so that we
can create that peaceful atmosphere in our home. And
unfortunately this knowledge does not come naturally.
Kids don't come out of the womb knowing how to deal
with conflict. It is a skill that needs to be learned. And it
will be learned, one way or the other. Without conscious,
wise, parental care the "skills" they are likely to learn are
violence and aggression or passivity and evasion. Kids

need to be taught how to enter into conflict and deal with it nonviolently, constructively, creatively, and responsibly.

TEACHING CONFLICT RESOLUTION

Example is a powerful way of teaching our kids to handle conflict. Kids tend to handle it the way they see us handle it. We often give examples without a lot (or any) thought of what we are doing. We will tend to respond to conflict the way we were taught to respond to it—with techniques learned from our parents, schoolteachers, peers, and the media. If we were taught to see conflict as a contest, we will probably fight physically or verbally with our "opponents" until one of us has won and one has been soundly defeated. If we saw our parents run from conflict, we will probably show our children how to run as well. If we were lucky enough to see significant people in our lives handle conflict assertively, without aggression or passivity, we can model for our children the same behaviour.

When given the proper tools, kids can and do come up with a productive plan to solve their own conflict. With young children you may have to give them options they can choose from. As they grow older, one of three things will likely happen:

1. They will share.
2. They will both get up and leave, finding something else to do.
3. One of them will come up with a plan they both agree to.

Telling and Tattling

It is important today that kids of all ages know when to tell and who to tell, and know that they will be taken seriously.

Tattling: If it will only get another child in trouble, don't tell me.

Telling: If it will get another child out of trouble, tell me. If it is both, I need to know.

If the distinction is taught to children when they are young, it can pay off in the teen years. Adolescents will understand that it is not tattling (or snitching) to tell you that their friend is giving away his possessions and saying subtle goodbyes to classmates. Telling may help get the troubled teen out of trouble. A friend is five months' pregnant and binding herself up in an attempt to hide her pregnancy. Telling might get her in trouble with some people, but it will certainly get her and her baby out of trouble. There is going to be a fight after school, and an arsenal of weapons has been hidden in the lockers of rival teens; telling will get kids in trouble in the short term but out of big trouble and serious regret in the long term. A friend is drunk and driving on a stretch of a major highway. Telling will get the friend in trouble and possibly keep him out of bigger trouble.

How we as parents respond to our children's telling will give them a clue as to whether they can safely tell us information that might be scary, ugly, frightening, or disturbing. You can start teaching three- and four-year-olds the difference between tattling and telling, using everyday events as opportunities to practise discerning when to tell and who to tell. As well as practising, keep the lines of communication open by being truly present and listening to what kids are saying, or trying to say, with their fumbled words, body language, and actions. Make no judgmental statements or threats. Just be there, aware, offering a "Tell me about it."

Time Out and the Teddy Bear

Instead of playing tug-of-war with the teddy bear, Dana grabs her brother's favourite bear and pummels her brother with it, because "I asked him for it nicely and he wouldn't give it to me." It's time to step in. Dana needs to learn that hitting is not an appropriate way of handling her anger. But she's certainly not ready to listen to her brother's side of the story or come up with a compromise they can both accept. She needs to cool off and deal with the results of her violence toward her brother. The tools she will need to use are the four steps of discipline, with the three R's being an integral part of the third step (help her find ways of solving the problem).

As a parent, you are there to help Dana calm down, fix what she has done, figure out how to keep it from happening again, and heal with the brother she has harmed.

You are quick to respond. "You are angry. It's okay to be angry. It is not okay to hit. You need time to calm down.

You can calm down in your room, in the rocker, or on my lap. Take your pick. Sometimes with older children, offering a choice between sitting and walking is also a good idea. Some people, kids included, can calm themselves more easily if they are moving about. The purpose and the intended results are the same: to calm down and then work through the original problem or conflict.

Once she has calmed down, the first thing she needs to do is fix what she did (Restitution). An apology is in order, but is requested, not demanded. If you demand an apology you will get one of two kinds: an insincere "I'm sorry" or the hit, obligatory "I'm sorry," hit again cycle. An apology is more likely to be forthcoming if the child has seen it modelled or has at some time been the recipient of a sincere "I'm sorry." Sometimes just offering a hug or a handshake says more than words can.

The second thing Dana needs to do is figure out how she can keep the incident from happening again (Resolution). She can't merely say, "I won't hit him again." That's what she won't do. She needs to know what she will do when she wants the teddy bear and her brother does not want to give it to her. It is during this step that you can talk with her about being aware of the consequences of her action—the impact it has on her brother (it hurts to be hit), the impact it has on her relationship with her brother (no one likes to be around people who hurt them; Matt might want to hit her back; he might become afraid of her; he might not want to share his toys with her ever), and the impact it has on her (hitting is a lousy way to play with other people, so soon she might have no one who will want to play with her). Dana needs to learn to stop between anger and the hit to look at more productive alternatives—in other words, to feel, think, and then act.

After Dana has figured out how to keep her aggressive outburst from happening again, she needs to heal with the brother she has harmed (Reconciliation). Through this step, Dana begins to understand that it is her responsibility and challenge to turn this event around, to help turn her brother's tears into a smile.

Double Trouble

Sometimes what you have on your hands is not just one kid hitting another but a genuine fist fight.

If two kids are hitting each other, I ask them to sit together, with me in between if necessary, or I ask them if they want to go away from each other to cool off. When they have calmed down, they can talk with each other about the feelings that led to the fight. Sharing their feelings will help them learn to be less quick to judge and more able to be compassionate.

A simple format kids can learn is:

When I heard (or saw) . . .	not When you said (or did) . . .
I felt . . .	not You made me angry
because I . . .	not I couldn't help it
I need (or want) . . .	not You'd better, or else

After both children have shared their feelings, guide them through the four steps of discipline:

1. Show them what they have done wrong.
2. Give them ownership of the problem.
3. Help them find ways of solving it.
4. Leave their dignity intact.

Then together they can come up with a plan for handling the conflict next time. And it will be a plan formed with a greater understanding of each other's wants, needs, feelings, and perceptions.

The Bully, the Bullied, and the Circle of Revenge

Sometimes a hit is not born of anger and frustration. A hit might arise from calculated and mean aggression: a sister holding her brother's arm behind his back and twisting till he screams in pain. Not playful teasing—"Joey has a girlfriend"—but taunting, circling a young boy in the school cafeteria, squirting him with ketchup and calling him a "fag." Not shooing a younger sister away because older sister is annoyed with her, but serious shunning: "Get away from us, you creep." Not two kids hassling one another with playful banter, but one child dominating the other in a relationship of victor-victim. Terrorizing, intimidating, tormenting, and shunning are behaviours that cannot be categorized as elements of sibling rivalry. They are behaviours of a bully, a child who hurts or frightens a smaller or weaker child deliberately and repeatedly.

Punishing the child will only teach him to be more aggressive and hurtful. And he will undoubtedly master the art of doing his bullying in ways that are sneaky or underneath the "radar" of even the most observant and aware adults.

Letting your child get away with such behaviour is no better. You are subtly telling him that you don't expect much more from him, thus giving him a ready-made excuse for being cruel or violent. ("I can't help it. I have a learning disability." "It's not my fault. I have impulse control problems." "I've got my dad's temper.") It is important that you not make light of the bullying and write it off as "boys will be boys" or "usual stuff" between siblings or playmates.

A child who bullies others typically

1. Finds it hard to see things from another person's perspective.
2. Treats siblings or peers as a means to achieve his own selfish goals.
3. Uses brute force or intimidation to get what he wants.
4. Is concerned with his own wants and pleasures, rather than thinking of others.
5. Tends to hurt his victims when parents or other adults are not around.
6. Views weaker siblings or peers as prey (bullying is also known as "predatory aggression"—a scary term to be sure, but not as scary as the actual behaviour it defines).

If you see your child displaying any of these traits, you must act immediately and decisively. Once again, it is time to use the three R's of reconciliatory justice: Restitution, Resolution, and Reconciliation. To work through this process you will also need to do five more things with the child who is doing the bullying:

1. Teach elements of empathy, and particularly perspective-taking. Challenge your child to walk in the other's shoes, to reflect on the other child's pain. Try to relate the pain to a pain that your child felt in a particular situation when he was upset, frustrated, or tormented.

2. Teach your child nonaggressive and peaceful ways to get what he wants.

3. Create opportunities for him to "do good." He needs opportunities to behave toward others in caring and helpful ways. In extending himself to others, this step also helps your child learn to notice and care about the rights and needs of others, which in turn helps him to practise the elements of empathy.

4. Closely monitor your child's TV viewing, video game playing, and computer activities.

5. Engage in other more constructive, entertaining, and energizing activities. Your child can attack a rock-climbing wall with the same fervour he once used to attack his brother. This time he will achieve a goal without "taking anyone out" in the process; he will feel a sense of accomplishment; and he can "do good" by

teaching his brother to climb the same wall. He can "cruise" the river looking for great rapids to conquer rather than "cruise" the school hallways looking for weaker kids to bully out of their lunch money.

Teaching a child to become assertive, not aggressive, to get his needs met in responsible, constructive ways, and to "do good" is going to take a great deal of time and effort on your part as a parent. It will mean taking stock of the way you get your own needs met, the way you handle minor and major conflicts in your own life, and the way you respond to your children's mistakes and mischief.

The Victim

A bully cannot be a bully all by himself; he needs a victim. If your child is the victim of a bully, don't count on him telling you about it in a forthright way. Victims are often ashamed of being bullied, are afraid of retaliation if they do tell an adult, and often don't think adults can or will help them. A deadly combination is a bully who gets what he wants from his victim, a victim who is afraid to tell, and adults who see bullying as teasing, not tormenting, as "boys will be boys," not predatory aggression.

The signs you can look for that might indicate your child is being bullied are:

1. An abrupt lack of interest in school or a refusal to go to school.
2. A drop in grades.
3. A withdrawal from family and school activities, wanting to be left alone.
4. Hungry after school, saying he lost his lunch or wasn't hungry at school.
5. Missing money and making lame excuses for where it went.
6. Torn clothing or missing clothing.
7. Using derogatory or demeaning language when talking about peers.

8. Not talking about peers and everyday activities.
9. Physical injuries not consistent with explanation.

If you suspect that your child is being bullied at school, inform school officials immediately. Keep good notes about the who, what, where, when, why, and how of any incidents of bullying. Follow up on the follow-through to make sure the adults are actively involved in protecting your child and any other child who is being bullied, and that the bully is not being punished or rescued but is in fact being disciplined.

You will need to help your child break away from the bully-victim relationship. Your first step is to respond to her expressed fears or the signs of being bullied with encouragement, support, and love. She needs to know she will be listened to, that nothing is too silly or ugly to be talked about, and that you are there as a caring adult to protect her. She needs to be aware that the way she responds to a bully influences the way he will respond to her. Remind her that aggression begets more aggression (responding in kind to a bully can escalate the potential danger of the situation); passivity invites aggression (cowering and giving in emboldens the bully to torment more); assertion can dissipate the other person's aggression (standing up to the bully might mean being wise enough to stand her own ground, walk away, or run as fast as she can to the safest place and to a trusted adult).

Creating a Caring Community

The tools for safeguarding your children from becoming victims of a bully are the same tools for safeguarding your child from becoming a bully. Add to these tools teaching perspective-taking, showing constructive ways to get needs met, and encouraging "doing good," and you have the ingredients for breaking up the bully-victim relationship, and for creating a caring community and safe harbour for all of our children.

If we are to survive as a planet, we must teach this next generation to handle their own conflicts assertively and nonviolently. It's going to take example, guidance, and instruction from us to impart to our children the wisdom of the peacemakers: violence is "the knot of bondage"; aggression only begets more aggression; passivity invites it; and assertion can dissipate it. Peace is not the absence of conflict. It is the embracing of conflict as a challenge and an opportunity to grow.

The Big C and the Three R's

Chores and leisure activity are the yin and yang of a strong personal and family backbone. The two cannot be viewed separately from each other, since the interplay between them creates a whole. A strong backbone that is at once stable and flexible cannot be developed by emphasizing one or the other. The backbone family seeks harmony and order individually and collectively through a dynamic balance of the two, viewing neither as superior to the other.

The greatest part of each day, each year, each lifetime is made up of small seemingly insignificant moments. Those moments may be cooking dinner, taking out the trash, stopping at a stop sign, relaxing on the porch with your own thoughts after the kids are in bed, playing catch with a child before dinner, speaking out against a distasteful joke, driving to the recycling centre with a week's newspapers. But they are not insignificant, especially when these moments are models for kids. And every time a child organizes and completes a chore, spends some time alone without feeling lonely, loses herself in play for an hour, or refuses to go along with her peers in some activity she feels is wrong, she will be building meaning and a sense of worth for herself and harmony in her family.

Chores

Getting kids to do household chores can be a chore in itself. Kids are more likely to do chores willingly if they feel that we truly need and welcome their help, that we are not simply giving them chores to teach them lessons or because we don't want to do the work ourselves. That means we have to present ordinary chores in such a way that they are meaningful to a child, useful for the family, and part of the harmonious order of our home—no easy task unless we ourselves begin to see ordinary chores in a different light.

Ordinary chores can help kids

- Develop the ability to organize their own resources
- Experience closure on tasks
- Organize themselves
- Set goals and build skills necessary to work through more complex physical and mental tasks

Children need to believe that they can make a contribution, can make a difference in their families.

If you want your children to learn a skill, do it yourself. Demonstrate for them first, then teach them. Guide them through it, and then let them do it on their own.

It is important that chores not be gender-biased. Boys and girls can and need to learn to mow the lawn, take out the trash, do the dishes, clean their rooms, do the laundry, cook, sew, use yard and shop tools, baby-sit, scrub the bathroom, pull weeds, plant a garden.

There are lots of ways to do chores. It doesn't always have to be my way. Be willing to give a bit. This is our home. We can do it in our way and in our time. Figuring out how to do this will mean communicating with one another, making our expectations clear, and listening carefully to one another.

Relaxation, Recreation, and Rebellion

If chores are one side of the yin and yang of a harmonious family structure, the three R's are the other. Relaxation, recreation, and rebellion may seem easier to deal with than chores, but for many people in our culture, "working" is actually a lot easier than "playing." In fact they may not even know how to enjoy leisure, and import the stresses and strains of their working style into their playtime. This is neither healthy for the adults nor good modelling for kids.

Relaxation—The Art of Meditation

We as adults are often uncomfortable being alone, quiet, and reflective, and we project those uneasy feelings onto our children. From morning to night we bombard ourselves with noise, talk, music, activity, constant movement, as our bodies and our minds cry out for rest and quiet. Quiet is not often encouraged or celebrated.

For children to grow in the sense of inner discipline, they need time to be alone and still. Taking the time every day to be still yourself will give you the opportunity to "be guided a little more by your gut." By encouraging your children to "sit down, be quiet, and get to like yourself," you will be giving them the opportunity to tap into their own intuition.

Recreating Ourselves
through Play

With a prayerful spirit comes a playful spirit. To see that spirit, watch a young child at play, spontaneously enjoying the moment without a worry about deadlines, rules, winners or losers, paycheques or bills. Play is more than the absence of work or the reward for work well done. It is not something that has to be earned. It is an opportunity to re-create and renew ourselves, and connect with others in the spirit of cooperation and acceptance.

Adults can and do turn child's play into rigid, judgmental, highly organized, and goal-oriented endeavours. The argument that we must teach children to compete in order to survive in the real world would be valid if the world we want them to survive in is one of dog-eat-dog competition. If our goal is to raise them to survive in the real world and make it a better place, it would serve us well to examine our cultural attitudes toward play, games, and organized sports. We can choose to raise our children to be competent, cooperative, and decisive individuals who, if they want to or have to compete, will do so with a moral sense.

Cooperative games are but one avenue for genuine play. Encourage your children to develop hobbies that they can get "lost in," go for hikes in the city or the mountains, swing on swings, run together, share a good movie, and most of all, laugh together. Let the chores and your work go for the time being. Get out with your kids for no other reason than to delight in one another's company. You will find that play can renew and refresh and reconnect each one of you.

Rebellion—The Art of Resistance

Just as chores and the three R's are the yin and yang in the formation of a strong personal and family backbone, relaxation and rebellion are both necessary to achieving a peaceful attitude. It is not enough to practise the art of meditation—to be alone and quiet, reflective and silent, cooperative and seeking harmony in relationships. To be wholly human is to balance this inner journey with the art of resistance.

Our children need to be able to see us take a stand for a value and against injustices, be those values and injustices in the family room, the boardroom, the classroom, or on the city streets.

We don't have to accept the status quo. We can make a difference if we are willing to acknowledge what M. C. Richards describes as "passionate priorities"—actively witnessing for the values we believe in, be they expressed in small deeds, simple gestures, or protest marches. When we do more than give lip service to our "passionate priorities," when we walk our talk, we model for our children ways to rebel and resist creatively, constructively, and responsibly.

The art of resistance involves both taking a stand and taking an action.

When Rosa Parks refused to give up her seat on the bus that hot day in Montgomery, Alabama, she was resisting a law that was created by one group of people at the expense of the basic human rights of another group. Her taking a stand helped create the momentum for the monumental civil rights movement in the United States. It was a small courageous act that gave witness to a "passionate priority" and changed the course of history.

REBELLION WITH A BIG I—INTEGRITY

Backbone families teach their children to go beyond standing up for their own rights while respecting the rights and legitimate needs of others. They teach their children the concept of "willing good"—that is, speaking and doing what is right, "even when the burden is heavy." It involves helping children to develop an inner moral voice (personal code) that guides them to do or say what is right, often in spite of external consequences and never merely because of them. This inner voice gives children the wherewithal to act with integrity when confronted with difficult situations, such as peer pressure intended to cause harm.

Money Matters

Since my children are not paid for everyday chores, I am often asked if I ever give my children money. Yes, I do give them an allowance for three reasons: to learn how to handle money, to make decisions about their own money, and to set financial priorities.

What is important for kids to learn is that no matter how much money they have, earn, win, or inherit, they need to know how to spend it, how to save it, and how to give it to others in need.

In deciding how much allowance to give our kids, we need to ask ourselves four questions:

1. How much can I afford?
2. How much do I want to give?

3. How much can my child handle? It needs to be enough not to frustrate the child but not so much that no responsible choices need to be made or priorities set.
4. What does my child need the money for?

Given the choice, children who don't want for anything will not save. And many children today don't want for anything. We have an obligation as parents to give our children what they need. What they want we can give them as a special gift, or they can save their money for it.

When charitable giving in the form of money becomes a habit, kids can then become aware of giving of their time and their talents as well.

When children start earning money for out-of-the-ordinary jobs at home or for work in the neighbourhood, they can start contributing to their long-term as well as short-term savings.

After giving and saving, the rest of the money may be spent on things that are not life-threatening, morally threatening, or unhealthy. You can allow a lot of freedom to a young kid to buy what is meaningful to her. When a child begins to recognize the difference between needs and wants, bare necessities, amenities, and luxuries, the structure for responsible money habits is being developed.

The backbone parent does not lend money frivolously and for every occasion but recognizes that there are times when any of us may need to take out a loan and repay it later.

When do you increase the allowance? Simple—when your kids can convince you that they need a bigger allowance.

You have a special problem if you have a wealthy or generous relative or parent who sends large sums of money to your children. This can undermine all the effort you put into teaching your kids to handle money. You can send a note to the relative or parent, along with deposit slips for your child's long-term savings account, and suggest, for the child's sake, that they send a small amount of money to the child and put the rest in the long-term account.

By constantly increasing the responsibilities and decisions our children have with their own money from the time they are toddlers, we can help make sure that by the time they leave home, they will be able to spend, save, and give in a caring, creative, and responsible way. It behooves us as parents to teach them well. Who knows, they might be managing our money someday!

Mealtime

There is something profoundly satisfying about sharing a meal. Eating together, breaking bread together, is one of the oldest, most fundamentally unifying of human experiences.

As food nourishes the body, food eaten in company also nourishes the individual spirit, the family, the community, and the world. The harmony of a meal eaten together spreads far beyond the table and far beyond mealtime.

Backbone parents provide a healthy and flexible structure for mealtime. It is a celebration, an occasion to come together as a family to nourish the body, mind, and soul. It is also a time to teach children about nutrition, food preparation, manners, and conversation or dialogue—the mutual exchange of ideas, opinions, and feelings. This doesn't mean that there won't be disagreements, as there are in any family, about what to eat, where to eat, how to eat. It's just that these disagreements are handled in a framework of reason and dialogue.

Reducing Food Conflicts

Food conflicts can be reduced by following a few simple guidelines:

- Have a variety of good foods in the house and eat those foods yourself.
- Teach your children about the food they are eating.
- Let your children help plan and prepare well-balanced meals and nutritious snacks.
- Eat a variety of meals served a variety of ways.
- At least once a month have a formal celebration with your children.
- Teach your children cultural or religious customs that have been in your families for years. And if you don't have any, create some of your own.
- Teach your kids manners, not etiquette. Manners are social graces that enable people to eat comfortably around one another; etiquette is adhering to rigid social rules and codified courtesies that often get in the way of people breaking bread together.
- Teach your children how to shop for groceries.
- Teach your children to cook.

Bedtime Doesn't Have to be a Nightmare

Don't lie to your children. Don't tell them they need their sleep. Be honest with them: you both need their sleep, and often you need more sleep than they seem to. You have to decide whether you want them to bed early and up early or to bed late and up late. As much as you might like it, you probably can't have them to bed early at night and up late in the morning.

Basically what has to be established is a *bedtime*, *bed place*, and *bedtime routine*.

As a family you have to look together at what works best in your home. Because of work commitments and your own body clock, you may prefer to have your young children have a late nap, be up with you later in the evening, and all of you sleep in later in the morning.

You have to do what you can live with, set what works for your family, and be open and flexible to the changing sleep needs and routines of the members of your family.

Backbone parents provide a basic bedtime routine that is flexible enough to adjust to the needs of the individual family members and the family as a whole. Responsibility for establishing the routine rests first with the parents, but then as the children grow older, responsibilities and decisions about bedtime and bedtime routine are increasingly turned over to them. By the time they leave home, the children have a healthy regard for the need to sleep, an understanding of their own body clock, and respect for the needs of those around them. In the give and take of family life they have learned common courtesies and are able to balance their own needs and wants with the needs and wants of those with whom they share living space.

Bedtime routines also need to be as individual as the families who create them. Kids count on some kind of consistency and some sort of structure. Basically they need to take care of their personal hygiene (face and hands washed, maybe a bath or shower, teeth brushed, toilet if necessary—usually advisable), change into bedtime wear (nowadays sleepwear can be more than just pajamas), do something calming to relax (singing, storytelling, reading, massage), dim the lights (some kids are like some adults and can sleep in the dark, and some are like other adults and need a small light on), and fall asleep.

If you do the routine with your toddlers, as they grow they will increasingly be able to do most of the routine themselves, forming good mental and physical habits as they become more independent.

Bedtime can be a wonderful time to hook kids on books, to fascinate them with animated sound effects, and to teach them about family history and traditions through storytelling.

Bedtime is a special time, a time of transition. It is an opportunity for closure to one day and a preparation for the next. It is a small turning point in the natural rhythm that gives structure and meaning to life. Just as the seasons and their holidays and celebrations mark the great natural movements of the years, so bedtime marks the turning of the days. With care and patience and awareness of our children's needs, each bedtime can be its own celebration of love and life.

Ready, Sit, Go—Toilet Training

A brick-wall parent takes ownership of the process of toilet training. She often wants to start the process before the child is physically ready. The child has learned to please in all other areas of life and will try to gain approval from her parent by being successful on the toilet, but after several accidents will become either frustrated or resistant, feeling like a failure or refusing to sit on the toilet at all.

A jellyfish parent has a laissez-faire attitude about the whole process. She provides little if any instruction on how the body functions. That a child might be ready to learn at two is missed by the parent because she doesn't see the signs, doesn't have the energy or patience to structure the task for the child, or is simply not there to provide the consistency, structure, support, and guidance. Inconsistency only prolongs the toilet-training process.

The backbone parent lets the child be in full control of her body functions and master her own toilet training at her own speed. The parent has a flexible routine, is positive and nonchalant about the routine, expects mistakes and sees them as opportunities to learn, has a relaxed attitude, and is available to help. She is not overly concerned about other adults' expectations and comments.

Both you and your child need to be ready to take on the task of toilet training. You need to be willing and able to give your child the time, patience, and encouragement she will need from you. And you need to know why you are helping her. Is it because you are tired of changing diapers, or the preschool won't take her unless she is toilet trained, or your neighbours' son sported training pants months ago? If these are the reasons, take a moment to think again. These might influence you, but the real question is, are you ready to help your child because she is ready to be helped?

THE THREE P's OF POTTY TRAINING

1. Prepare
2. Practise
3. Patience

Once you and your child embark on the toilet-training adventure, thanks to your willingness to establish a backbone structure of preparedness, practise, and patience, your child will be able to begin to see herself as a competent, resourceful, and responsible person who is learning to treat her own body with dignity and regard.

Sexuality is Not
a Four Letter Word

Kids learn about their sexuality even if it is not us doing the teaching. But often what they learn is misinformation and misinterpretation, exaggerations, and exploitative notions about their own bodies and bodies of people of the opposite sex.

If we want to be the primary sexuality educators of our children, it is critical that we begin an open communication about sexuality early in our kids' lives so that a positive pattern of communication is established before the hormonal changes of puberty affect our teenagers' thoughts and feelings about their own sexuality.

With the understanding that sexuality is much more than sex, as parents we can convey with verbal and nonverbal messages that our sexuality is a wonderful part of our total being, not just what we do with our genitals. Our actions and expressions, our emotions, the way we treat our own bodies and our children's bodies, the way we respond to their cries and react to their basic bodily functions—all these help our kids to develop healthy attitudes about their own sexuality, as well as help to create a comfortable environment for our children to get to know their own bodies and ask questions.

Backbone parents begin to lay a strong foundation for raising sexually healthy children even before their children are born, by coming to understand their own sexuality and how it is an integral part of their values, morals, emotions, and sexual feelings. This strong sense of self enables backbone parents to celebrate the beautiful qualities of both boys and girls without stereotyping the sexual roles of their individual children. It also becomes a model for children to emulate. Treating your own body, your spouse's body, and your child's body with dignity and respect is the beginning of a lifelong relationship of trust, caring, and nurturing.

As your young children begin to locate and explore all of their own body parts, you can begin to establish an open and honest channel of communication by using the proper names for all of the body parts. Using slang allows us to walk around the subject of sexuality rather than talk directly about sex organs and their functions.

Teachable moments are simple, ordinary, everyday situations that present opportunities for teaching your young children about sexuality. They present opportunities to impart knowledge, values, and a moral backbone on which your children can build their own sense of themselves as sexual beings.

Girls tend to begin their physical and sexual growth spurt at eleven or twelve, boys at fourteen or fifteen, and emotional development for either can occur before, after, or simultaneously with the physical growth spurt. It's no wonder that the most pressing question is "Am I normal?"

Preteens need to know the detailed facts about sexuality, intimacy, dating, and sexually transmitted diseases. The more knowledge they have now, the better able they will be to make responsible decisions about the expressions of their sexuality later.

It is during the "un-age" (ages twelve through fifteen) that the drive to separate from their parents is taken up in earnest. At the same time adolescents are looking for your approval, support, and guidance. This age is punctuated with raging hormones and simple questions that have complicated answers. Your teen will probably be wondering about falling in love, crushes, self-pleasuring, homosexuality, intercourse, and issues related to wet dreams, periods, and pregnancy.

It is between the ages of sixteen and nineteen that your teens will move toward independence in all areas of their lives. No longer seeing you as their parent, they look to you as a mentor and guide when it comes to issues such as responsible and respectful sexual behaviour. Issues that have been touched upon before now command stage front and centre:

- Sex—why is something so natural and good so complicated?
- Abstinence—the only sure way to avoid pregnancy and sexually transmitted diseases. Are there other benefits?
- Gynecological exam—what is it and when should I have one?
- AIDS and other sexually transmitted diseases—causes, prevention, signs, and symptoms. Can I trust her if she says I am her first?
- Contraception and safer sex—can the two be mutually exclusive?
- Love and sex—can you be in love without having sexual intercourse?
- Sexual abuse—what is it and how can I avoid it?
- Intimacy and friendship—what's the difference and can I have both?

As they move on into adulthood, they will assume full responsibility for their physical, spiritual, moral, and sexual growth. You will remain a mentor and begin the wonderful process of becoming their friend.

危機

Parenting through Crisis: Helping Kids in Times of Loss, Grief, and Change

As a parent, I have suffered in ways that I never imagined. Others who have suffered inconsolable losses have shared their stories with me. In living through our losses and in sharing our stories, we all discovered that, although each one of us lives through a solitary grief that is our own, we are not alone in our suffering, nor are we the only ones to suffer such a grave loss. We all knew this to be true in our minds before we went through the chaos. Living through it, we now know it to be true in our hearts and our souls as well.

It is our wit and our wisdom that help our children, and us, through the passages of grief. It is in our grieving that we learn a new wholeness. It is in this wholeness that we are able to embrace our sadness, knowing that it shares space with a quiet joy and a gentle peace.

Life Is Not Fair, Life Hurts, Life Is Good

These three seemingly incompatible expressions are really three parts of the whole of living. They are threads woven through the tapestry each one of us creates as the visible expression of our being a part of humanity. To accept these three is not to abandon hope or optimism, or to deny our real grief. To accept them is to rid ourselves of the unnecessary suffering that comes from struggling against these three truths and trying to make them something they are not.

Whether we are dealing with a death, an illness, an accident, a divorce, or mayhem, we will need peace of mind, optimism, and resolve to handle the chaos, the loss, and the suffering that come hand in hand with each of these. How we handle our mourning will give our children tools to handle theirs. When we offer them our compassion and empathy, we give them, from our own tapestry, strong threads of hope and resolve to grab on to and eventually weave into their own rich tapestry of life.

TAO of Family

Tao is the Zen Buddhist word for "way" or "path." It is not a source or an absolute. In and of itself, it yields no truth or answer. It is not the way or the path. Like an algebraic formula, Tao is both empty and useful; and like a formula, it can be used again and again in many different situations. Such is the TAO of Family. It is a path and a way.

TAO of Family is also an acronym for the three things we need when our lives are thrown into chaos: Time, Affection, and Optimism. These three form the foundation for all of the other TAOs in this book. TAO of Illness, TAO of Divorce, and TAO of Hope—each has its own unique formula, its own way or path. But they all start with time, affection, and optimism.

Time

When we are consumed with grief, it is often difficult to find time for anything except our own grieving. We hope our kids will see our grief and understand. Understand, maybe; accept, probably not. We need to find time for our kids, even if it is time to share in the grieving, lest they become the hidden mourners.

Spending time with our kids can help them handle their own mourning. We also need to give them time to get through their grieving. There is no way to rush grief, condense it, or eliminate it. If we don't give kids the time now, they will need to take the time later. Grief doesn't just go away.

We need to take time to be silent, to think, reflect, and just be. Our children also need that time. And we need some quiet time together, to be still in our grief: willing to be present and not act. In stillness we can be more aware of a bigger picture. Sometimes possibilities that didn't present themselves in the midst of a crisis come forward during the still moments. And sometimes possibilities that didn't exist at the moment of the crisis come together to create a better resolution than was even possible in the first hours, days, or weeks of a loss. In our stillness we can be open to those possibilities.

Affection

Our children need a smile, a hug, and humour every day. In times of grief, these three are often cast aside as a grey cold heaviness descends upon the house. But it is these three that can help all of us get through our mourning. A smile, even one we had to work hard to create, lifts our spirits. Hugs let us know we are in this together. A hearty laugh is contagious and can provide a respite from our grief. With these three simple gestures we give our children all three parts of the TAO of Family—our time, affection, a sense of optimism—and we do it with little thought or effort. Which is a good thing, because thought and effort are usually in short supply when we are grieving.

Optimism

Optimism is a grateful attitude, a willingness to view even adversity and adversaries from a fresh perspective.

Optimism doesn't deny anger, frustration, sadness, or intense sorrow. It is willing to give each one its due, but only its due. We cannot always control what happens to us, but we can control how we respond to it and how we use it.

To accept realities for what they are, to look at ways to use those realities for good, and to get busy solving the problems created by those realities help us reaffirm our optimism.

Every time we reaffirm our optimism, we give our children a good way to approach their own adversity. They can take an active part in determining what they will do with what life has handed them. They will be less likely to be passive recipients of whatever comes their way. They know how to view change, be it welcome or unbidden, as a challenge and an opportunity to grow.

Triangle of Influence

In times of chaos, if we are going to respond to our own suffering and our children's grief in an active, self-aware, compassionate way, we will need to use our minds, our hearts, and our intuition together. To rely exclusively on any one of these to get through the suffering is to narrow our perspective, limit our options, and hamper our grieving.

When either mind or heart works independently of the other, the denial, repression, hatred, blame, and worry created rob us of peace of mind, our sense of optimism, and the resolve we need to face our suffering and heal our pain, and help our children do the same.

It is our intuition that can bridge the two seemingly disparate perspectives. Being able to acknowledge, trust, and act on our intuition is particularly useful when we are faced with complex difficulties, major chaos, and profound loss. It can point a way out of an impasse that thinking and emotions have created by doing battle with one another. It often provides options that aren't immediately obvious to our mind or our heart. When we connect our head and our heart to our intuition, we are no longer just logical or just emotional. We no longer merely react. We become mindful with a wise heart.

Our intuition helps us to know when to reach out and when to refrain from reaching out; when to speak and when to be silent; when to hold on and when to let go. In a small or large crisis, we are able to respond with a generous spirit, wisdom, discernment, empathy, abundant kindness, mercy, and compassion.

Death: Helping Kids Mourn

Confronting the reality of death honestly and directly with children is difficult at best. In a death-denying, fix-it-fast, cure-it-now society, with so many rituals and customs of our ancestors abandoned or never experienced, the task is even more painful and necessary. Our own feelings, belief systems, faith traditions, questions about mortality and the meaning of suffering, as well as our understanding of the abilities of children to handle loss and grief, can help or hinder us in helping our children mourn. We can try to hide the loss from them, try to shield them from the anguish, convince ourselves they are too young to under-stand—they will still grieve, but without the comfort, support, knowledge, and tools they need.

There are things you can do in advance of a death and during the passages of grief that can help both you and your children journey the uncharted waters of your loss.

The Circle of Life

Before they face the death of a family member or friend, children are helped if they first learn about death from everyday events such as the changing of the seasons, a dead bird in the yard, the death of a family pet. Observing life cycles in everyday living, and talking about them matter-of-factly, can be one kind of preparation for the inevitable deaths of loved ones.

It is easier to explain the basic attributes of death and answer the inevitable questions calmly and forthrightly when we are ceremoniously burying the dead robin than when we are grieving at Grandpa's grave.

All children who experience the death of a family member feel helpless and lost. At all ages and stages of development, children have ways of coping with loss. Even when they are too young to understand the concept of death or speak what they are feeling, they are able to grieve.

Four Attributes of Death

Children as young as five can begin to understand what Elliot Kranzler describes as the four attributes of death (text in parentheses added by author):

1. It has a specific cause (nobody just "drops dead").
2. It involves the cessation of body functions (the body can't move, can't feel, can't breathe, can't grow—it's not just sleeping).
3. It is irreversible (it can't be undone, there are no "overs").
4. It is universal (it happens to all living things).

Path Through Grief

There is no destination, no arrival, no ending place in the journey of grief. There is no road map to follow, no formula, and no way to hurry the journey or bypass the pain. There are passages to live through, not stages that we move past in a lockstep, hierarchical order. To force ourselves or our children into a linear grieving "process," evaluating where we are on the ladder of grief, is a vain attempt to control and manipulate a "journey of the heart." This journey cannot be controlled, it can only be lived through by each one of us in our own time and in our own way.

The path we each will crawl, walk, run, stumble through, sit down on, and at times try to run from will be our own. Others can tell us of their own journey, where the potholes were, the ruts, and the resting places, what they carried and what they discarded, wished they had brought along, or found in hidden stashes along the way. In the end it is up to each one of us to travel our own path, naming our loss, honouring our grief, confronting our pain, and telling our story.

THE PASSAGES

As we journey through our many losses in life, there are three passages that we experience over and over again:

1. The piercing grief of goodbye
2. Intense sorrow
3. Sadness that shares space with a quiet joy and a gentle peace

When someone dies, we and our children, all in our own time and in our own way, need to go through these passages if we are to choose "an acceptance of death and a commitment to living." There is no one way, no right way, no only way, no singular journey. We can share our path with others, but in the end it is up to each one of us (our children included) to create our own path.

It is important to remember that these passages are fluid and overlapping. All three can, one by one, barge into our lives unbidden and without notice. They don't always take place in a set order and all can be present in the same day.

1. THE PIERCING GRIEF OF GOODBYE

This first passage is marked by numbness and shock. The body mercifully provides us with these two to help us slowly face the impact of our loss. We might feel as if we are walking in a dream state, appear to others as being stoic or robot-like. We are often in denial, hoping to wake up from a nightmare, searching the papers or listening to the news, fighting, against all odds, to learn that it isn't true. The first words out of our mouth—"Oh no"—are a frantic attempt to change what is.

During this time it is important to give shelter to one another as each of us individually, but also as part of a family and a community, slowly continues the circle journey from the depths of piercing grief to intense sorrow, a passage that has its own elixirs and its own dragons to slay.

2. INTENSE SORROW AS WE REORGANIZE OUR LIFE

The mind is no longer on hold, the reality of the death is seeping into the very marrow of the bones, the numbness is wearing off, a dull, constant pain taking its place. The sorrow envelops your mornings, evenings, and nights, allowing no respite.

The nightmares of the first passage give way to the logistics of everyday routines, routines that are the same and yet irrevocably changed, now coloured stone-cold grey. Even happy times bring you sorrow. You can't reason the pain away. Nor can you rush through this passage or deny it its due. The sorrow needs to be expressed.

You and your children need to speak of the loss, tell your stories over and over again. Be as patient with your children's stories as you wish your friends and relatives would be with yours.

It takes courage to get through this passage, to not deny it, inhibit it, or rush it. You will find if you confront the pain honestly and directly and you are open to its lessons, you will increasingly feel the desire to let go of the intensity of your grief and get on with your own future.

3. SADNESS THAT SHARES SPACE WITH A QUIET JOY AND A GENTLE PEACE AS WE RECOMMIT TO LIFE OURSELVES, TEMPERED BY THE LOSS AND WISER

Not feeling bad for feeling good is a sign you are moving into the third passage of grief. Tired of being tired, ready to get on with your life, and no longer preoccupied with despair, you laugh more and are able to concentrate better. No longer plagued with the "Why?" that has no decent answer, you move on to "What will I do now?" You've said your goodbyes, you've restored yourself, and now you are ready to reinvest in your own life. The sadness is there, but it shares space with the quiet joy and the gentle peace.

Your children might move into this third passage before you or after you. They need your support and reassurance that it is good to get on with their lives. Let them know that getting on does not mean forgetting, trivializing, or getting over a major loss. It means always remembering, honouring the relationship that is there, and knowing that one does not get over a major loss, but gets on with life.

Humour

Humour is potent medicine for the heart, the body, and the soul. It releases tension and provides us with energy to deal with feelings that could easily overwhelm us. It is life-affirming. We are all grateful for people whose humour in a time of loss can give us a jump start at reconnecting with life.

The wit that helps us through a funeral—that same wit that helps us get through our two-year-old's artwork on the newly wallpapered wall, the sandwich in the VCR, and the strangely tinted laundry—might take a turn toward the humourously absurd when we are face to face with death and its aftermath. Those around us who haven't yet found their own funny bone, or who wish us to handle grief in a solemn, prescribed, or at least dignified manner, will be stunned, shocked, and aghast at our gallows humour.

Breaking the News

When faced with the death of a loved one, and confronted with your own grief, there is no easy way of getting through breaking the news. Use simple, honest words: Daddy died; your sister was killed in a plane crash; Grandpa died last night; your aunt killed herself. Honesty doesn't have to be cold and harsh and unfeeling. Your tone of voice, what you say, and how you say it can speak warmth, caring, and sadness.

Often parents feel they have to soften the blow by beating around the bush before they get to the fact of the death. No amount of talking, theologizing, rationalizing, or confronting will ease the pain. Your children need gentle honesty and caring silence. Stick with the headlines and facts, then be present to hold your children, cry with them, and answer any questions they might have. They might be shocked and unable to do anything but cry, or too shocked to even cry. They probably won't be interested in lots of details; just let them know you will be there for them if they have any questions. Assure them that together you will make it through this.

Euphemisms, Platitudes, and Proclamations

All three are attempts to soften the blow. They don't. In reality, they are hidden stashes of denial and avoidance that mask the truth, keep death obscured, and in vain try to smother the pain. They are covers for our own unease with death and our self-doubt about what we claim to be feeling. They only increase confusion and fear.

EUPHEMISMS

"Daddy passed away."
"Your brother has gone to the light."
"Grandpa passed over."
"We've lost your sister."
"Your aunt is sleeping."
"He's gone to his final resting place."
"He's moved on."
"She's with your grandmother."
"Your little brother has gone on a long journey."
"God wanted your mother."

PLATITUDES

"It was for the best."
"God only takes the best."
"Only the good die young."
"You are only given what you can handle."
"Think of what you have to be thankful for."

PROCLAMATIONS

"It's God's will."
"You should be glad that your brother is no longer in pain."
"She's in a better place than we are."

Factors That Influence Children's Grieving

Since a family has members of different ages, at different stages of physical, emotional, and intellectual development, who have different relationships within and outside of the family, no death the family faces together will have the same effect on everyone. Five factors greatly influence children's grieving:

1. Who died and what relationship that person had to the child
2. Manner or cause of the death
3. Communication skills of the family
4. The history of loss and death
5. The developmental level of the child

When Grieving Is No Longer Good Mourning

Sometimes grief is blocked, diverted, or buried. The following is a checklist of warning signs that your child might be stuck in grief and need professional help to get through mourning. All children will exhibit some of these signs as they grieve. It is the frequency, intensity, and persistence of these behaviours that indicate a need for concern.

____ 1. Acting much younger for an extended period of time.

____ 2. Excessive and prolonged crying bouts.

____ 3. Inability to sleep or need for excessive sleep.

____ 4. Nightmares or night terrors.

____ 5. Loss of appetite.

____ 6. Extended period of depression in which child loses interest in friends, daily activities, and events; putting a negative spin on events.

____ 7. Truancy or a sharp drop in school performance and grades.

____ 8. Prolonged fear of being alone.

____ 9. Persistent idealization of the dead person.

____ 10. Excessively imitating the dead person.

____ 11. Repeatedly stating the wish to be with the dead person.

____ 12. Clinging to the past and refusing to think positively about the future.

____ 13. Talking about the dead person in the present tense.

____ 14. Overvaluing or clinging to possessions of the dead person.

____ 15. Frequent physical complaints, illness, headaches, stomach aches.

____ 16. Detachment and pulling away from efforts at consolation.

____ 17. Avoidance of any activities that might be a reminder of the dead person.

A Journey of the Heart: Acute Illness, Chronic Illness, and Disability

The journey of the heart that each one of us takes as we face the death of someone we love is the same journey we will take when someone in our family is diagnosed with an acute illness, a chronic illness, or a disability. The three passages that we circled through—the piercing grief of goodbye, intense sorrow as we reorganize our life, sadness that shares space with a quiet joy and a gentle peace—will become well-worn paths that we will travel over and over again. Occasionally we will meet our children going in the opposite direction; sometimes we'll travel with them hand and hand. And sometimes we will be ahead of them, wishing they would catch up, only to find out they have already been there, done that, are ready to get off and end their journey as we must continue on in ours.

Acute Illness and
Chronic Illness

An acute illness—such as chicken pox, meningitis, strep, ear infection, pneumonia, or appendicitis—can cause exceptional stress on a family for a short period of time. By definition, acute illness is sudden, brief, and severe. It can be a wake-up call to remind us of the gift of good health that we take for granted when we are well. It can help us put petty problems into perspective. Acute illness can also bring us to our knees in grief if our child dies or is seriously handicapped as a result of complications.

A chronic illness is of long duration and/or recurring. It can cause minor or major stress on a family for a long time, and sometimes for a lifetime. Its cause is not always apparent: a real-life tragedy with no known villain. It is often invisible. It can radically change family routines, rituals, and traditions that were in place long before the illness became a permanent fixture in the home.

Chronic illness is more likely than an acute illness to affect your child's psychological and social development. Extended absences from school and extended trips to the hospital can exacerbate moodiness and a sense of social isolation. Your child's role in the family might change markedly, especially if the chronic illness results in a permanent disability. Six of the most common chronic illnesses that affect children today are asthma, severe allergies, arthritis, diabetes, seizure disorders, and cancer.

An illness can be either acute or chronic depending on its severity or the duration of treatment. Cancer can be an acute illness that is severe, short in duration, and deadly, or severe, short in duration, and curable. It can also be a chronic illness such as leukemia, requiring long-term treatment and the possibility of recurrence.

Both acute illness and chronic illness can cause a mental or physical disability that can have a small impact on a child's life or a large impact on the entire family.

Passages of Grief in Acute and Chronic Illness

I. PIERCING GRIEF OF GOODBYE

When a diagnosis has confirmed what our mind and heart already suspected or hoped was not true, we are thrown into the shock of this first passage. We might try to deny the truth; it does no good. We might rage at the doctors, at the gods, at life itself. We are in a state of disorder and disbelief. We numbly go through the routines of the day, not remembering how we got from one place to the next. We look in medical journals to find the exception that does not exist for our child, the cure that has not yet been found. Hopes and dreams are dashed, and it is too soon to be optimistic about new hopes and new dreams.

The goodbye of death is final. This goodbye keeps on going, like a nightmare that relentlessly intrudes and refuses to be chased away with wishes or bargains. In death there are rituals and routines that help us put closure on the event. This is not true with an illness. There are no rituals, only medical routines and therapies, new medicines and checkups, diagnoses, treatments, and prognoses. We have to find closure before we can move on. Often that closure is the acceptance of the diagnosis. This acceptance is not a resignation or a giving up of the fight, it is the naming of the beast. In that naming we have the power to create our story, granted with a character we didn't invite and whose lines we would rather not hear.

2. INTENSE SORROW AS WE REORGANIZE OUR LIFE

As we begin our new story, we move into a time of deep sorrow. The full impact of the diagnosis and its implications hits us. We have little energy for the ordinary tasks of life, and now must add therapies, medicine, trips to the doctor's office and hospital. We want to be dormant, to pull into ourselves and escape from the everyday realities of the illness or disability. The *what if?*s are driving us crazy. No longer numb, the mind keeps rolling back time to the moment before the accident, the day before the illness, the night our child was conceived, struggling against reality to re-create a different ending.

But we can pity ourselves for only so long; our bodies and minds need to move out from under this sorrow. It is time to busy ourselves with creating a new identity that includes the illness or disability but is not totally framed by it. It is a time to step back and gain a new perspective. It is also a time when we can reach out to someone else in pain, knowing we have travelled a similar path.

We can find ourselves stuck in this passage if we are unable to get any respite, if we are in an unending cycle of intensive caregiving. Our child will be stuck in this passage if the illness or disability consumes her every waking moment. Sometimes the treatment or therapy needs to take a back seat to everyday events or a trip to the park.

3. SADNESS THAT SHARES SPACE WITH A QUIET JOY AND A GENTLE PEACE AS WE RECOMMIT TO LIFE OURSELVES, TEMPERED BY THE LOSS AND WISER

As we begin to re-energize, we can feel ourselves wanting to laugh and be released from sorrow's burdens. We welcome the new energy and the ability to concentrate on something other than the disability or illness. We don't feel bad that we feel good. We know that we have been through the valley of darkness and have come out on the other side, changed but very much alive. It is not a matter of getting over the losses that the disability or illness creates. It is knowing that we can get through the pain and the grief. Only people who have known a great loss can really know the quiet joy and gentle peace of this passage.

Knowing we can get through the pain and the grief does not keep us from returning to the first and second passages when we are hit by a new loss, or when an old loss comes back to haunt us. It's just that once we have been through the third, we know it is a place we can find again.

In this journey of the heart, the circle that directs us back to the present moment with all its possibilities, we won't find answers; we can find a new perspective, a new way of seeing.

The Language of Illness

Just as there is no easy way to tell your child about a death, there is no easy way to tell your child about an acute illness, chronic illness, or disability. The formula is the same: headlines first, facts next, and delete the editorials.

After the headlines and facts, be present to your child to hold her and field as many questions as she needs to ask. She might not want to talk right away, she might be too shocked and want only to be alone. She probably won't be interested in much detail, but be prepared in case she is. Assure her that you will get through this together. Diagnosis, treatment, and prognosis can be explained simply as three questions:

Where am I at? (diagnosis)
Where am I going? (prognosis)
And what do I need to do to get there? (treatment)

The language you use with your child will depend on her age and intellectual ability. Keep it simple but truthful. Use the medical terms along with simple explanations or drawings.

Language is a powerful tool: it can help your child create a positive, powerful self-image or it can relegate him to an illness-based identity. A child who has diabetes is a diabetic; a child with epilepsy is an epileptic; a child with asthma is an asthmatic. It takes a bit more effort and a few more syllables to say the former instead of the latter. It is worth both more effort and more syllables to keep from defining a child by his illness or disability. Avoid the shorthand and open your eyes to the whole child before you: he might have limits because of his illness, but he is not limited to his illness.

TAO of Illness

The TAO of Family got you through the everyday events in life when life seemed so normal. The TAO of Mourning got you through the trauma of a death. Death had a finality to it, its shock mercifully one swift blow. This trauma goes on and on, with new nightmares more vivid than the old. Hopes are raised and dashed; good news simply cloaks the bad news. As much as it seems that these two TAOs have run out the door along with the friends and relatives who don't know what to say or do, they are not gone. You relied on them before when you were at a loss for what to do. They are still there for you to lean on when your mind seems like mush and your heart is full of pain, when your children are scared, fearful, jealous, confused, or embarrassed. The three universal moral qualities—wisdom, compassion, and courage—will join these two to become the TAO of Illness, your road map through what seems to be an endless minefield.

The Journey for Siblings

The journey of the heart for your child who is ill or disabled is not a solo run. His brothers and sisters are along for the ride whether they want to be or not. Not only must they rise to the challenges of growing up, they must also deal with the many challenges they are presented with because they have a sibling who is ill or disabled. The usual sibling rivalry will be there, but it will be amplified, in part because of the amount of parental attention the one child will need for her treatments, trips to the doctors, or extended hospital stays.

Teach your children to communicate with one another and to settle their differences themselves, with you as their mediator and guide. Accent the individuality of each of your children. Let them come to know one another as brothers and sisters with their own unique strengths and weaknesses. The wisdom, compassion, and courage possessed by your child with a disability or illness are there for her siblings to possess as well.

Divorce

Divorce can be a courageous act or an act of cowardice, or not a choice at all. It can be something that is thrust upon you and you must somehow accept. Divorce can be good for you; it can be bad for you. It is often ambiguous. But for children it is a time of great chaos and loss.

Children don't choose a divorce, and they have little control over what happens to them during and after the divorce. They can't control the contact they will have with either parent. The continuity they have come to depend on might be radically altered by a move, by a change in employment of one or both parents, or by financial hardship. The losses are real to children and need to be acknowledged by adults. Kids are resilient, but just because you are elated to be out of a soured marriage, don't expect your children to rally on as if this were just a minor change in their lives.

No two divorces are alike. The impact a divorce has on children has much to do with the maturity, good sense, and goodwill of the parents, as well as the age, emotional and psychological maturity, and gender of the children.

Parental conflict during the divorce process, and parental abandonment after the divorce process, plus poverty, financial loss, school relocation, in accumulation, can have the most profound and devastating effects on children. It is our responsibility as parents, family members, friends, and community to minimize the accumulation of these risk factors for any child experiencing the myriad losses that can surround parental divorce.

We can begin to minimize the losses by individually reaching out to offer our presence, concern, and a listening ear; by offering divorce mediation and child advocacy to bring children's rights and needs to the table; and by establishing community programs to help parents and children.

The Beginning of the
End of Marriage

The *why?*s of a divorce are not the issue here. Marriages end for many reasons: we were not adequately prepared; we were unrealistic in our expectations; we were madly in love with an emphasis on the madly, not love; the relationship became destructive physically or emotionally; one partner in the marriage fell out of love and into a new love with no effort to address the problems in the first marriage; one partner abandoned ship; both partners realized the marriage was an impulsive mistake, or both felt a good divorce was better than a bad marriage. When children are involved, it is important that we rise above our adult differences, act with integrity throughout the divorce process, and make a concerted effort to minimize the accumulation of the risk factors that can compound our children's mourning.

Common Questions

Some of the most common questions are:

- Where will we (the kids) live?
- Where will Mom live? Where will Dad live?
- Who will keep me safe?
- Will we go to the same school?
- Who gets the dog?
- Will we get to see Grandma and Grandpa?
- Will we be poor?
- Who will take care of me when I am sick?
- Who will take me to piano lessons?
- When will I see Mom (or Dad)?
- Who will sign my permission slips and my report card?

Why?

Older kids may ask the *why?* of the divorce. Save the gory details and dirty laundry for your adult friends, counsellors, and therapists. You can be truthful without being hurtful or casting either parent in a negative light. If the question is about the other parent, an agreed-upon response can be: "We have agreed not to answer questions on the other parent's behalf. It's okay to ask your dad [mom] about it directly." Remember, the two of you are getting a divorce, not the kids. The kids need to have a meaningful and healthy relationship with both parents.

The next *why?* is often "Why can't you work it out?" You might or might not have a respectable answer for that one. However, you can assure your kids that, despite the many issues you could not work out in your marriage, one thing you will make work out is a decent coparenting arrangement. The marriage has ended, the family has not. All of you will be bound together as family, sons and daughters, mom and dad. In the future, the family tree might become a family forest, but even in the forest each branch of this tree will always be connected to its original roots, its family of origin.

If your kids don't ask questions, you can bring things up when you sense they might have an unspoken fear or concern about what is happening. Listen carefully for comments that might contain questions they are afraid to ask.

Don't be afraid to be repetitive. What children might have blocked out at the onset of their grief will be listened to and understood at a later time. As children grow older, in an effort to make better sense, emotionally and intellectually, of what they have gone through, they will likely revisit the events and the emotions surrounding the divorce. It's not that they didn't get it the first time; they are now able to think about and process the information at a different level, with a different perspective, and more clearly.

You can let them know that you are truly sorry for the hurt that the divorce will cause them, and that you will be there for them to share that hurt. Don't say, "I know how you feel," because you don't. You know how you feel. You can show them empathy, not pity or sympathy, by looking at things from their point of view. You can assure them that they have every right to be angry, upset, hurt, and bewildered. They even have the right to feel relieved that the tension they have sensed in the household for so long is finally gone.

The Facts

Whether they ask or not, kids need to hear over and over again:

- They still have a family.
- They will have two homes, one with Mom and one with Dad.
- Both parents will always love them and take care of them.
- The kids did not cause the divorce. This is an adult problem.
- They will not be left in the dark about any decision that will affect them. Their feelings will be acknowledged and considered. However, the adults will make the decisions, based on the children's best interests.
- They will never be asked to choose one parent over the other, to act as a messenger or as a spy.
- They will not be treated as another piece of property to be fought for, bargained over, or seized.
- They will have the financial support of both parents.

Kids' Passages of Mourning

1. PIERCING GRIEF OF GOODBYE

"Oh no. This divorce isn't really happening." During this time kids will do everything they can to deny the reality of the divorce. They will lie to their friends and teachers about what is going on at home. They will try to convince themselves and younger siblings that their parents don't really mean it, or are sure to change their minds. They might also express anger and rage at anything and everything. Schoolwork usually suffers, with kids lost in daydreams, distracted, or so angry and frustrated that they are unable to concentrate on anything but the reality that their world is being torn apart. If parents are doing battle at this point, children might exhibit extreme hostility or aggression.

2. INTENSE SORROW AS THEY REORGANIZE THEIR LIVES

Kids often become lethargic at this point, just barely moving through life. Every major and minor change reminds them every day that the divorce is not going away. It is playing out in 3-D right before their eyes and they are powerless to stop it. Some children will try to be very good or overly helpful. Others will try to rewind this horror movie by setting up ways to force their parents to get back together.

3. SORROW THAT SHARES SPACE WITH A QUIET JOY AND GENTLE PEACE

Special events, a schedule of dates at Mom's house and dates at Dad's house, memories, and photographs still bring pangs of sadness. However, if parents have been able to carry out a decent coparenting plan, have resolved their differences without hostility and vengeance, and have allowed their kids to express their feelings and opinions freely and honestly, kids will see that they still have two parents who love them and have their best interests at heart. Their enthusiasm for life will return, and they will be able to redirect their energies into all of the normal activities their own growing up entails.

TAO of Divorce

As we go through the painful process of the separation and divorce, we need to be present to our children with time, affection, and a sense of optimism. It takes time to teach children to handle their feelings in a way that will serve them well. It takes our affection—that smile, hug, and humour every day—along with our unconditional love. Kids need to know it is all right to feel. It is okay to be happy, concerned, joyful, sad, angry, frustrated, and hurt. Their feelings do count.

Though they have been brought to their knees with grief, they know they can survive this loss, people will be there to help them get through their grief, and they do have the power to choose their own way to respond to it all. With optimism they recognize that they can't always control what is happening to them. What they can control is how they use what is happening to them.

Add the six critical life messages

- I believe in you.
- I trust in you.
- I know you can handle this.

- You are listened to.
- You are cared for.
- You are very important to me.

To the TAO of Mourning add restraint, kindness, and intelligence:

RESTRAINT: the biting of the tongue, the holding back of the invective and accusations, letting go of the need to get even or win at the other's expense.

KINDNESS: the benevolence, consideration, generosity, tenderness, and thoughtfulness needed to overcome the bile of bitterness that eats at the lining of the heart.

INTELLIGENCE: the discernment, the wisdom to look beyond the vantage point of the earth beneath our own feet and courageously embrace the whole, leaving behind judgmental comments and legalistic righteousness.

The Language of Family vs. the Language of Dysfunction

Words are powerful tools, and the language of divorce needs to be cleaned up if we are to truly help our children develop a strong sense of self. Without even thinking about the connotations of words and their impact on children, we say that they are from a "broken home" and the "victims of divorce." The phrase "she's from a single-parent home" is often used, not to describe the make-up of the family system, but rather to explain, excuse, or validate a flaw in the child's behaviour or performance.

The words we use to express this attitude tend to isolate parents and their children, brand them, undermine their sense of self, family, and parenthood, and connote second-class status worthy of pity or condescension. Adversarial language that is harmful and degrading perpetuates the suspicions our culture has about family systems that are different from the "nuclear family" or "family of origin." By simply changing certain everyday words we can improve our own and our children's sense of identity, sense of family, and sense of belonging in a community. A change in language can help us move on to a life that acknowledges the divorce as a part of our past, but refuses to let it put a stranglehold on the present or the future.

Simply changing the language does not eliminate the hurt and the pain all of us must deal with when there is a major change in our lives. Changing the language doesn't negate the fact that a divorce has taken place; it does not deny the realities of the temporary loss of structure and stability and perhaps status that existed in the marriage. It does not deny the chaos and confusion our children faced. We've experienced a great loss. But once we've mourned that loss, it will not serve us or our children to constantly define ourselves only in relationship to that loss.

OLD LANGUAGE	NEW LANGUAGE
• broken home	• my family, two-home family
• failed marriage	• marriage ended
• custodial parent/ noncustodial parent	• parent, mom, dad
• joint custody	• coparenting, shared parenting, shared responsibility
• sole custody	• primary responsibility
• children are visiting their dad	• the children are with their dad, with their other family
• custody and visitation	• live with, be with, stay with
• access	• parenting time

- real family
- ex-wife, ex-husband

- child support

- family of origin, nuclear family
- children's mother or children's father; helps focus on the parent–parent relationship you will continue to have, not on your former intimate relationship
- contribution

—From *Mom's House, Dad's House*, Isolina Ricca

Options for Constructive Solutions to Divorce Disputes

Regardless of how you and your marriage partner related or didn't relate in the marriage, during the process of divorce you will need to talk to one another, make decisions, put piles and piles of information together, and discuss the next twenty years of your children's lives—all of this when neither of you feel particularly civil, friendly, talkative, organized, clearheaded, or receptive to the other's presence. In his book *Integrity*, Stephen L. Carter sets out three steps that can be useful in helping the two of you do what is right and just, not necessarily what you are legally entitled to do, obligated to do, or want not to do.

1. Discern what is right and what is wrong.
2. Act on what you have discerned, even at personal cost.
3. Say openly that you are acting on your understanding of right and wrong.

These three steps will not provide clear-cut answers for you. They are like the TAO of Family: they can provide a formula for both of you, even with your anger and hurt, to work together with integrity to resolve the complex issues facing you and your children.

Legal Tools Available

The three legal tools available in divorce disputes are, in descending order of civility and ascending order of cost, mediation, arbitration, and litigation. If used exclusively to resolve all of the issues, the first will enable you to establish a workable coparenting arrangement, but might not adequately address complex property and financial issues; the last used alone will guarantee that you get what you are legally "entitled to" and that both of you will be working for years to pay your legal bills, and even longer to repair the emotional rifts created by the cycle of retribution and retaliation that litigation can invite.

It's possible that you will need to use all three of these options as you sort out your different personal, material, and financial arrangements. In order to discern which option to use when, you will need first to separate the major decisions about your kids from decisions that need to be made regarding money and property. Attend to kid issues first and let these issues be the overriding factor in any decision you subsequently make about property and money. In the heat of battle, it is easy to want to do just the reverse, try to settle the property and money issues and then use the kids as clubs to beat the other parent into giving in or giving up.

This is the time to let go of the need to "win" on principles and work toward what is in the best interest of the kids.

Coparenting Plan

The same philosophical tenets of parenting can become your philosophical tenets of coparenting:

1. Our kids are worth the time, energy, and resources it takes to come up with a coparenting plan that demonstrates both parents' commitment to do the right thing for the kids. We have a clear sense of direction and purpose.
2. We will not treat the kids or their other parent in a way we ourselves would not want to be treated. We will be honest and fair.
3. Whatever we do will leave the dignity of all parties intact. We are willing to compromise, to agree to disagree, and to confront one another assertively.

It is possible to end your marriage and create responsible, civilized, active two-household families if you are willing to reduce the acrimony between one another and remain involved in your children's lives. Not every divorcing couple has the trust, respect, and ability to communicate with each other to make a coparenting arrangement work. But for the sake of the kids, it is worth investing your time, energy, and patience to try to create a coparenting plan.

The process itself can help the two of you remain focused on your goal of minimizing the accumulation of risk factors that can have devastating consequences for your kids, and maximizing the opportunities to allow your kids to develop strong, loving relationships with both parents. In the beginning you might not actually be co-parenting. Parallel-parenting might be more like it, as each of you tries to disengage from the other and begin a new chapter in your own life, apart but forever connected as parents by and to your children.

There are legal and personal issues involved in developing a long-term coparenting plan. A mediator can help the two of you create a plan to meet your individual family's need. But a mediator can only help. You would be wise to reflect, in advance and often, on the following issues:

- Basic philosophical tenets that each parent espouses.
- Your individual and joint parenting goals.
- Responsibilities each of you are going to assume.
- Decisions each of you are going to be expected to make.
- Responsibilities the children are going to be given, and by whom.
- Decisions the children can make.
- Resolution of present and future disagreements. (It is helpful to have a Plan A and a Plan B for this one.)
- The risk factors to the kids and ways each of you plans to minimize them.
- The outer limits of tolerance in the coparenting plan, i.e., what each of you can live with, can't live with, could tolerate, don't mind, and don't you even ask.

Families Born of Loss and Hope

For many years, the definition of "family" has been debated and batted around by many diverse groups. The debate is often tainted with moral absolutisms and ideological biases, and the definition generally ends up being more exclusive than inclusive. To get hung up on what is the best kinship structure is to deny the variations that have served us well throughout history, in different times and places, in different cultures, and through great chaos and loss. To define the family as only one type of kinship structure is to define others as aberrations or deviations, not "real" families.

Stepfamilies, foster families, single-parent families, and adoptive families are no more and no less "real" than the one that is traditionally spoken of as the "family of origin," "natural family," or "biological family." The three characteristics of family hold true for a family of one child and one parent, two biological parents and two children, two stepparents with his, hers, and ours, parents and adopted children, grandparents raising their children's children, four generations living together, and any number of variations on each of these combinations.

A family is:

1. A small group of people bound together by commitment, caring, and cooperation, traditions, common rituals, and common language, whose boundaries are identifiable, firm, and flexible.
2. A microsystem in which each member is affected by and affects other members and the system as a whole.
3. Part of a larger community (macrosystem) that interacts with and influences the family and its individual members (social, economic, and political).

A new baby is born, a teen goes off to college, a father dies, a grandparent moves in, a daughter marries, a foster child is adopted. All families form, grow, shrink; they change in structure, function, and interaction through the marital, parental, and kin relationships that are integral to the family system. These relationships are by their nature dynamic, interconnected, interactive, and reciprocal. The family in its essence continues and constantly redefines and renews itself.

Complications and Complexities

No family is without its complications and complexities, its losses, boundary ambiguities, communication barriers, commitment concerns, and discipline hassles. Being aware of the ones unique to your kinship structure is step one in helping you avoid the pitfalls that can undermine your family.

1. LOSS

Death, divorce, infertility, adoption—the losses involved in each plunge adults and children alike into grief. This grief cannot be denied, refused, overlooked, minimized, or belittled. It must be named and faced head on. If the family born of the loss is to thrive, the three passages of grief (piercing grief, intense sorrow, and sadness that shares space with joy and peace) need to be honoured, not rushed or cast aside.

2. BOUNDARY AMBIGUITY

"Who's in and who's not?" "Who's the parent and who's the kid?" "Whose parent and which kid?" "What's appropriate, what's not?" These simple questions address the issue of family boundaries. In families born of loss and hope, the answers can be complex and conflicting.

3. COMMUNICATION

In order to relate to one another, we need a relevant language and lines of communication that are available, open, and direct. Language helps define who we are as individuals and in relation to one another. It is difficult to tell our story when there is a paucity of language or when the language is steeped in negative definition. We stumble over the half-sister, stepbrother labels and then try to explain the biologically related sibling: saying she is my "real" sister implies that the others are in a less than "real" relationship.

Lines of communication are too often severed in divorce, convoluted in stepfamilies, sometimes open and sometimes shut in adoption, shut down completely or shrouded in secrecy in the case of NRT (New Reproductive Technology). For any family to communicate well, it must be able to create its own history and its own stories around that history.

4. COMMITMENT

Creating a family takes time and commitment from all involved—commitment to one another and commitment to the family as a functioning entity in and of itself. Commitment involves certain rights, responsibilities, and obligations that go beyond, yet may be bound by, law (in the case of stepparents, adoption, and NRT, legal protection doesn't always exist).

5. DISCIPLINE

For the most part, in one kind of family, the discipline issues around mealtime, bedtime, sibling rivalry, chores, and getting your teen out of jail are the same as in any other kind of family. The need to have limits and boundaries, rules and consequences, and to follow through is no different in a family where all members are biologically related than in a family where some children are biologically related to the parents, some adopted, and some in foster care. The ages and stages are the same; the purpose of discipline (i.e., to give life to learning) is the same; the steps are the same; what is different is history—where each person involved in the process is coming from and what the history of the relationship between the parent and the child is at the present.

TAO of Hope

Just as any family that is born of loss and hope is, by its nature, complex and complicated, so is its TAO. To find the TAO of Hope, take the TAO of Family (time, affection, and a sense of optimism), add the three passages of grief (piercing grief, intense sorrow, sadness tempered with joy and peace), the TAO of Mourning (including the six critical life messages), and the TAO of Divorce (acting with kindness, restraint, and intelligence), multiply them all by the number of family systems involved, and add compromise, generativity, and balance.

Compromise, the act of adjusting or settling by mutual concession, will become second nature to you as time passes, if all adults involved in the various family systems are willing to embrace generativity. Generativity—"devoting our time and energy to the nurturing of the next generation as opposed to being fully absorbed in our own lives and pleasures" (Erik Erikson)—is a critical element that all adults involved in a family born of loss and hope must factor into their decisions and interactions. To make such a family a safe harbour for children, the rights, needs, and wants of all parties need to be balanced against the final weight of what is good, just, and right for the children.

Adoptive Families—a Brief History

In the early 1900s it was common for a family friend, neighbour, or relative to raise a child who might or might not have contact with her biological parents. Family boundaries were often quite fluid and functional.

In the mid-1900s, adoptions became more formalized, with parents and children connected through doctors, lawyers, and social workers. There was a concerted effort to match the physical characteristics of the parents and children so that they could be seen as a biologically connected family. These were often "secret" adoptions.

By the late 1940s, with an emphasis on the primary importance of the "nuclear family" and the stereotyping of such families through the media, the secrecy, stigma, shame, and institutionalization of adoption became entrenched through state and provincial laws. Birth records were sealed and new birth certificates were issued listing the adoptive parents in place of the biological parents.

By the 1960s, children adopted under these statutes were reaching their late teens and early twenties. Some began to search for their biological parents, often with the support of their adoptive parents. Biological parents, many of whom felt "forced" to place their child up for adoption because of their age, family shame, cultural taboos, or societal pressures, began to seek information about their child's well-being or seek contact with the child.

By 1980, both sides of the adoption equation were changing. On the front end, "open adoptions" were being tested both formally and informally. Who could adopt and who couldn't was being challenged. Interracial adoptions were being proposed and opposed. News accounts of children in need of adoption in Poland, Romania, and China opened one more avenue for adoptive parents and allowed some to escape the challenges of "open adoption," only to replace them with the different challenges of "international adoption."

On the back end, records were being unsealed. Adopted children and their biological parents could choose to register with various groups, hoping to make contact with one another through a mediator. Not only were the pros and cons of open records being debated, the debate was playing out in living colour in many living rooms. Secrets, stigma, shame, silence, hidden photos and letters, liaisons concealed were like skeletons rattling around in closets for far too long, finally pushing open the door and falling out on the floor for the knowing and unsuspecting alike to see. Issues faced by stepfamilies for generations were now spotlighted for all parties concerned: titles, names, histories, holidays, traditions, rituals, graduations, weddings, visits, grandchildren, and inheritance.

Today, with as many variations on the theme as existed in the early 1900s plus the added elements of transracial adoptions, multicultural adoptions, international adoptions, single-parent adoptions, and varying degrees of open adoption, the adoption process is forever changed. But the emotional, physical, and psychological needs of the child who was adopted have not.

The Language of Adoption

What we call ourselves and what we are called can greatly influence who we become. *Adoptive Families* magazine has published a list of terms considered hurtful to participants in adoption, along with recommended alternatives:

OLD LANGUAGE	NEW LANGUAGE
• real parent, natural parent	• birth parent or biological parent
• adopted child, own child	• my child
• illegitimate	• born to unmarried parents
• give away, place for adoption	• make an adoption plan
• reunion	• meeting, making contact with
• adoptive parent	• parent
• search, track down parents	• to locate, contact
• an unwanted child	• a child in need of adoption
• hard to place	• child who has special needs
• foreign child	• child from another country
• is adopted	• was adopted

The language doesn't deny the reality of the adoption, nor does it eliminate the loss, hurt, and pain that must be dealt with because the adoption happened.

Ages and Stages

A child's adoption will influence her emotional, psychological, and social development. How you as a parent deal with the issues of loss, grief, confusion, anger, and identity can aid or hinder her development in all these areas. Sometimes you will need to guide and speak, at other times watch and listen. Open, honest communication, a willingness to go over and over the issues as your child gradually absorbs the complexities of adoption, and an acceptance of your own grief and your child's grief will help your child grow up with a strong sense of self, a strong sense of family, and knowledge that she is loved.

Throughout the various ages and stages, your child will learn to attach and to separate. The tension between separation and attachment is often amplified in a child who is adopted. There can be a tendency to hang on to others for fear of being abandoned, or to isolate himself so as not to risk hurt and rejection. This tendency can be minimized if you and your child can develop a strong bond, trust one another, and communicate openly and honestly.

Twice upon a Time:
Stepfamilies

No other kinship structure has been reviled, scrutinized, attacked, stereotyped, and mythologized more than the stepfamily. Though sometimes called the "stepchild of the real family," structurally flawed, impaired, a poor imitation of the real thing, opposite of intact family, it is none of these.

The word "step," in this context, comes from the Anglo Saxon word "stoep," meaning bereavement or loss. All stepfamilies are born of some bereavement or loss.

Years ago, most stepfamilies were formed following the death of one of the parents. Today they are formed as the result of divorce or death or two single/adoptive parents by choice.

The basic characteristics of a stepfamily are:

- It is born of loss.
- At least one spouse is a stepparent.
- The family system is complicated and multidimensional.
- Not everyone is necessarily happy about the marriage.

A stepfamily is a real family that will often take at least three years, and sometimes more, to feel like a family linked together by a combination of love, commitment, biology, and memories. Its creation is a slow and, at times, methodical process with all the ups and downs of any kinship structure. Added to the mix are myths and fairy tales, name games, the question of whether or not to adopt, teens and the potential for sabotage, sexuality in a sexually charged environment, and children of his, hers, and ours.

Myths

Most of the myths surrounding stepfamilies are unfounded, false notions that need to be dispelled.

1. The myth of instant love: The expectation that a stepparent will immediately love her stepchildren because she has fallen in love with their father can put a strain on the entire family. There is no such thing as instant love. It takes time, patience, shared memories, and a shared history for love to develop.
2. Stepparents will love their children and their stepchildren equally: Loving and caring are not about equality, they are about relationships, all of which are unique and not conducive to comparisons.
3. All problems are directly related to being in a stepfamily: Not true—some are and most aren't. Most problems are related to being in a family, and would be there regardless of the kinship structure. To frame every problem as stepfamily-related is to seek a simplified excuse for complicated interpersonal interactions.

4. Stepfamilies will do everything the same as the family of origin: They can't and they shouldn't try. A stepfamily is a new kinship drama with a new cast of characters, new scenery, new script, and no director to coach the players. It is a comedy, tragedy, and mystery rolled into one.

5. There is a best time to create a stepfamily: There is no best time, though some times are easier than others. Creating a stepfamily with teens is not easy and can be very complicated. However, there are pluses and minuses at all ages and stages. That includes the ages and stages of the adults as well as of the children involved.

6. A stepfamily is far better than a single-parent home: Even the reverse is not true. Staying in a single-parent home can have as many pluses and minuses as creating a stepfamily (just different pluses and minuses). Both work best when they are seen as viable kinship structures and not as a way to avoid the alternative.

The Name Game

What we call ourselves and one another speaks much more than the name itself. It tells us who we are to ourselves, to our families, to our community. Names connect us to one another and at the same time make us distinctive from everyone else. They can show our position in a family, reflect respect, show love.

Names can also present a problem. Just as it takes time for stepfamilies to truly function as a family unit, the names they call one another need to evolve over time. And just as stepfamilies need to make a conscious effort to create rituals and routines and traditions, a conscious effort needs to be made to discuss the issue of names.

Children need to pick a name for their stepparent that is comfortable to use and that the stepparent can live with; "extra mom" or "pretend mom" won't cut it. It's important that both parents let the children know that it is okay to practise lots of alternatives, but rude or disrespectful names are out of the question. It is just as important that a stepparent not demand to be called "Mom" or "Dad."

Surnames are another concern in stepfamilies. Stepsiblings close in age have to answer a lot of questions and do a lot of explaining when they have different surnames. Some families use the various surnames on legal documents and a singular surname for all other documents and activities.

Adopt or Not

Where it is an option, some families have decided the best way to solve the problem of different surnames and create a strong stepfamily is for the stepparent to adopt the stepchildren. This could be a solution to a lot of problems besides the surname. A young stepchild who has no contact with her biological father could well benefit from being adopted by her stepfather. If the biological parent has died, the adoption can help the child feel more rooted in the family. The ceremony and the ritual surrounding the adoption can help strengthen the bond between the stepparent and stepchild, and the family as a whole. It is also the only way currently to create a legal bond between the stepparent and stepchild. (This is beginning to change with new laws and statutes that recognize the various kinship structures.)

There are three other reasons why adoption could be beneficial for all parties concerned:

1. Medical consent: Adoptive parents have the power to make medical decisions for the child; this is not automatic for a stepparent.

2. Inheritance: A stepchild has no right of inheritance unless the proper legal steps are taken beyond a simple will. Adopted children share equal rights to inheritance with the biological sons and daughters.
3. Custody rights: If the biological parent dies, the adoptive parent will retain legal custody of the child. Stepparents, regardless of the length of the relationship or the strength of its bond, have no custody rights.

There are more reasons why adoption might not be a good solution to what is now a stepparent/stepchild relationship:

1. Inheritance: If you adopt your stepchild, she might be relinquishing her rights to the inheritance from her biological parent.
2. Custody rights: If the marriage "goes south," you don't get to. As the adoptive parent you are legally and financially responsible for your adopted children, even if the children resent your involvement in their lives.
3. Money: Once you legally adopt your stepchild, all support payments from the biological parent are gone.
4. Abandonment: Perhaps the most crucial reason the adoption question needs to be thought through carefully is that with adoption comes the other side of the equation: abandonment. Unless the biological parent is dead, that parent must relinquish all rights and

basically sever his or her parental relationship with the child. This might be a good thing if that is what the parent has in fact already done. However, it could also mean that the child must deal with the fact that, just as you are willing to adopt him, someone else is willing to abandon him. The emotional costs might be much higher than the many benefits of adoption.

Adoption is not a cure-all for stepparent/stepchild woes. It will not make a bad relationship better, and it could make it worse. It can also make a good relationship even more solid than before. It is one of those situations where the TAO of Hope can point the way. The adults need to be willing to compromise, to practice generativity, and to balance their rights, needs, and wants against the final weight of what is good, just, and right for the child.

Reasons a Solid Stepfamily
Is Good for Teens

1. Stepfamilies can be healthier than the families of the first marriages, as long as all of the adults involved are willing to learn from the problems in the first marriage, leave most of their excess baggage behind, and make a concerted effort to compromise, embrace generativity, and create a safe harbour by balancing the rights, needs, and wants of all parties against the final weight of what is good, just, and right for the kids.

2. When parents are happy it benefits teens. Spousal conflict in first marriages can do a lot of harm to kids. Being free of the conflict allows kids to spend energy on handling the normal conflicts in their own lives. A stepfamily can be a place to get a fresh start and create new memories. It can also be a role model for a good marriage and instrumental in helping teens develop the ability to form good love relationships.

3. As long as a stepparent is willing to be present, but not overbearing, to be a mentor and a guide, that teen will have one more positive role model and one more supportive, caring person in her life. It's impossible to have too many loving people in your life.

Most adults in stepfamilies and therapists who work with stepfamilies agree that the most difficult time to attempt to form a stepfamily is when teenagers are part of the mix. Teens are apt to try to undermine everyone else's hard efforts to make the family work. The three most difficult issues to deal with when it comes to teens and a stepfamily are attachment/separation struggle, history, and sexuality.

Sexuality—Yours and Theirs

Put newlyweds together with a bunch of kids of all different ages and stages of sexual development, blur the boundary lines of relationships, add communication problems, commitment challenges, and discipline, and you have a stepfamily facing the challenge of creating a sexually healthy family in a sexually charged environment.

Intimacy and sexuality are different in a stepfamily than in a first marriage. In this second time around, you often have an audience of children who are curious about their own sexuality and embarrassed by the openly affectionate display of yours. Your teens are also embarrassed about the changes in their own bodies and would really rather you not behave the way they want to.

Stepchildren might be attracted to the stepparent, the stepparent to a stepteen, and stepsiblings to one another. Usually in the biologically connected family the boundaries between affection and sexuality are clearly defined; the children and parents have a history together of physical touching that is natural and innocent. Physical affection, bantering, and jest are a normal and welcomed part of their relationship and the relationship with siblings. This history is not there in newly formed stepfamilies.

The sexual and emotional maturity of the adults is paramount if the children are to get the help they need in respecting the healthy boundaries of romance and sexuality. Both adults must be committed to promoting the sexual well-being of everyone in the family. Open eyes and open communication are vital. When anyone in the family expresses an uncomfortableness, listen and be aware. The uncomfortableness could be a red flag that something is amiss.

If there is any risk for abuse, or if the family is breaking apart emotionally because of an overly sexually charged environment, get help fast. It is much easier to prevent sexual problems from growing into family crisis than it is to try to repair the damage once the lines have been crossed and boundaries violated.

His, Hers, and Ours

Dreams are dashed, hopes are buried, positions of status surrendered, jealousies resurface, relationships forever altered—and we're talking here about the birth of a child into a family, a child wanted by at least two people in that family, and the only one related to everyone else in it. When a child is born into a stepfamily, it is a monumental event that creates monumental changes for all the other children. As excited as you are to be the proud biological parent again or for the first time, your children and/or stepchildren might not immediately share in your excitement and bliss.

It must be for a heart reason that you choose to have a child together. You can factor all the pluses and minuses and still not come up with the right answer. Listen to children's free advice on the matter, but don't ask them for permission.

As parents, you have a chance to reevaluate your attitude and behaviour toward all of the children. Becoming a biological parent for the first time can help make you an even better stepparent. The rituals and traditions surrounding the birth of this child can help create stronger family ties and boundaries. It's a joyous moment when you hear your other children announce to their peers, "We have a new baby!" Even the jealousy the step-siblings feel can help them draw closer to one another as they try to make peace with this new enemy in the camp.

Effective Childrearing

Effective childrearing is one of the primary goals and one of the most perplexing problems for any family. The key is to believe that you are a family first, with some unique aspects as the result of being a stepfamily, single-parent family, or adoptive family. By concentrating on creating a healthy emotional climate at home—in the face of adversity, chaos, loss, sibling rivalry, financial struggles, another trip to the dentist, a call from your former spouse's lawyer, and inevitable conflict with your present spouse—you will find that you have the resolve it takes to make your particular kinship structure a truly effective family.

A new family can be a new beginning for all members. No one has to keep doing what they have always done, or do what was done to them. The key is to recognize the messages and tools you received from your own parents and are still carrying around; become conscious of the messages you are giving your children directly or indirectly; and become aware of the emotional and physical environment you are creating as a family.

Mistakes, Mischief, and Mayhem

How we respond to our children's many mistakes, occasional mischief, and rare mayhem can help provide the wherewithal for our children to become responsible, resourceful, resilient, compassionate humans who feel empowered to act with integrity and a strong sense of self, or to become masters of excuses, blaming, and denial who feel powerless, manipulated, and out of control.

Whether they feel empowered or powerless will greatly influence their ability to handle the myriad traumas they will experience throughout their lives, traumas brought about through death, divorce, illness, natural disaster, broken friendships, loss of a job, or mistakes, mischief, and mayhem they create themselves.

Punishment, Rescuing, Discipline

For mistakes, mischief, or mayhem that intentionally or unintentionally create serious problems of great consequence, the three R's of reconciliation are incorporated into the four steps of discipline. These three R's—Restitution, Resolution, and Reconciliation—provide the tools necessary to begin the healing process when serious material or personal harm has occurred. Whether it is only the four steps or the four steps and the three R's, discipline deals with the reality of the situation, not with the power and control of the adult. It helps change attitudes and habits that might have led to the conflict, and it promotes genuine peace in the home.

Discipline involves intervention to keep a child from further harming himself or others, or real-world consequences, or a combination of the two. Real-world consequences either happen naturally or are reasonable consequences that are intrinsically related to the child's action. Discipline by its nature requires more energy on the part of the child than on the part of the adult. If a consequence is RSVP—Reasonable, Simple, Valuable, and Practical—it will invite responsible actions from the child. If it isn't all four of these, it probably won't be effective and it could be punishment disguised as a reasonable consequence.

Often such disguised punishment is predetermined and is based on the assumption that all violations are clear-cut. Violations are subject to a one-size-fits-all punishment, regardless of the intent of the violator. In our rush to swift and certain judgment, there is no place for discernment of intent; the deed is seen only as a violation of a rule. Even a mistake unpunished is looked upon as a possible misstep down the slippery slope to more violent deeds. Such a mentality of zero-tolerance creates an environment of zero-options for parents. It is a simplistic response to complicated actions. It wrongly presumes that a young offender created the mayhem with the foresight, judgment, and maturity of an adult.

The opposite extreme (punishment's alter ego) is rescuing a child because we believe that children are incapable of wrongdoing with malevolent intent. We make light of the incident, ignore it entirely, or make excuses for the behaviour. If we don't draw attention to it, maybe it will just go away. This is just as wrongheaded as the punitive approach. Overcome by the sympathy we feel for the perpetrator, we try to convince ourselves that if we only knew the why of the child's misdeeds and the history that preceded the mischief or mayhem, we would be compelled to forgive and forget. Punishment ignores intent; rescuing ignores the severity of the deed.

Discipline is a more constructive and compassionate response that takes into consideration the intent, the severity of the deed, and the restorative steps needed to give life to the child's learning and to heal relationships that might have been harmed. It invites us to respond to our children with mindfulness, reason, a wise heart, compassion, and mercy, instead of just reacting with logic or emotion. It enables all of us to go beyond mere repair to restitution, resolution, and reconciliation.

During times of chaos and loss, it is children who have experienced such discipline, instead of punishment, who will have an inner reserve or resource to draw on when their strength is sapped, their intellect assaulted by the answerless questions, their emotions thrown into turmoil by raw, piercing grief.

Nonviolent Engagement and Reconciliatory Justice

When youngsters create mayhem intentionally, or through their mistakes and mischiefs at home or in the community, neither harsh punishments nor full pardon will heal the victims or the perpetrators of the mayhem. It is nonviolent engagement that is at the heart of true reconciliatory justice: the willingness to confront wrong-doing and reach out to the wrongdoer. It refuses to allow us to divide our world and our relationships into "us" and "them." It denies us the myopic vision that limits our insight. It reminds us of our connectedness with one another and can point the way out of an impasse that bitterness and hatred have created.

In *Prisons that Could Not Hold: Prison Notes 1964–Seneca 1984*, Barbara Deming, a civil rights activist, speaks about how ". . . nonviolence gives us two hands upon the oppressor—one hand taking from him what is not his due, the other slowly calming him as we do this." The one hand keeps the offender from causing more harm to self or others; the other calms down the offender, allows time for reflection, and invites reconciliation. As our two hands reach out, there is at once an attempt to bring about a balance and a tension created that keeps both parties actively engaged in the reconciliatory process as we strive to heal the rift created. We are attempting to restore community.

When a mistake results in serious harm, our arm of compassion reaches the farthest, while the arm of mindfulness helps the child acknowledge what has happened, confront the feelings of sadness, guilt, and fear, and take responsibility for the action, as well as rise above what has happened and get on with her life.

When mischief results in mayhem, the two arms are extended equally. Compassion and mindfulness are both equally needed.

When a child commits intentional mayhem, the arm of mindfulness is the longest at the beginning of the reconciliatory process, while the arm of compassion is still there.

The end goal in all three instances is an embrace in which the kids take responsibility as is warranted, are willing to make restitution, resolve to keep the mischief and mayhem from happening again, and commit to once again becoming active participants in the community. In the embrace, we are ready and willing to have them as participating members of our community.

For the youngster whose mistake or mischief has resulted in serious damage or harm, we might be inclined to offer only the arm of compassion. This will deprive the child of any opportunity to heal from within. She is likely to beat herself up emotionally, psychologically, and perhaps physically for the harm she has caused and can't fix.

How young offenders are treated will influence what kind of people they will grow up to be and what kind of lives the rest of us will live. If we don't help them reconcile with the community, we could well condemn ourselves to a lifetime of fear, distrust, and mayhem.

When an entire community is committed to reconciliatory justice, young offenders are invited to rise above their misdeeds and violent acts. The goal is to mend and restore rather than isolate and punish. The search is not for vengeance but for ways to heal people and heal relationships.

Forgiveness

Forgiveness is not a verb, nor is it an act of the will. Forgiveness is the voice of the heart that speaks the presence of the soul. It is heart business—the mind will be busy enough working out ways to demonstrate the forgiveness through deeds, actions, releasing debt, and making real the tangible expression of forgiveness.

Reconciliatory justice is a visible expression of forgiveness and the act of healing in a community. It is perhaps the one tool that can begin to cut through the chains of violence. It does not excuse the violence, does not deny the dignity and worth of the victim or the humanity of the oppressor. It does justice to the suffering without perpetuating the hatred. It is the triumph of mindfulness and compassion over vengeance and retribution.

Life Lessons

Parenting through Crisis took almost two years to write. The stories are true. The lessons are universal and bypass cultural differences, language barriers, and borders. Suffering and loss are inevitable elements of life.

Recent events have once again made real the seemingly incompatible expressions that are three parts of the whole of living: life is unfair, life hurts, and life is good. Also shown in living colour were the three passages each one of us circles through on our journey—the piercing grief of goodbye, the intense sorrow as we reorganize our lives, and the sadness that shares space with a quiet joy and a gentle peace as we recommit ourselves to life, tempered by the loss and wiser. Once more we saw that bigotry, hatred, fear, and fanaticism have a human face, and can cause just as much, if not more, suffering, pain, and grief as do the inevitable losses in life.

Only time will tell if the life lessons in such tragedies will be taken to heart. Will we point fingers, place blame, fortress our homes, schools, communities, seek revenge, and hold hostage another generation to the manacles of bigotry, hatred, and intolerance? Or will we, as individuals and an entire community, do what is necessary to take weapons out of the hearts, minds, and hands of our kids? Will what we learn help us to create more caring, more compassionate, less alienating, less violent communities where our children can know that they are welcomed as responsible, resourceful, resilient, contributing community members—each and every one having worth simply because they are children?

In this time of great chaos and suffering, can each casualty be given a human face? Can we reach out to others with compassion and empathy, honouring our deep bonds and common humanity?

Can a deep passion to alleviate another's pain and sorrow become a part of our everyday life? Can we reach out to our neighbours who are suffering their own personal tragedies and ask: "What are you going through?" "What do you need?" "What can I do?" Can we be there for them as they name their loss, honour their grief, confront their pain, and tell their story?

When we respond with a generous spirit, wisdom, discernment, abundant kindness, and mercy, when we help alleviate the suffering of others and we offer them our compassion and empathy, we create caring communities and safe harbour for our children.

Notes